CH

Everything I Never Learned in School about How to Be Successful

by

Darin Colucci

Everything I Never Learned in School about How to Be Successful
Published October, 2016

Editorial and proofreading services: Kathleen A. Tracy, Karen Grennan
Interior layout and cover design: Howard Johnson
Photo credit, front cover: Sneakers on cracked concrete surface with painted arrow
pointing in two different directions, Image ID: 301659998, Shutterstock

 **SDP Publishing**

Published by SDP Publishing, an imprint of SDP Publishing Solutions, LLC.

For more information about this book contact Lisa Akoury-Ross by email at
lross@SDPPublishing.com.

ISBN-13 (print): 978-0-9977224-7-5
ISBN-13 (ebook): 978-0-9977224-8-2

Library of Congress Control Number: 2016953366

Copyright © 2016, Darin Colucci
Printed in the United States of America

This book is dedicated to my wife, Lorna, and my son, Jackson. Both of you bring me more joy than I can adequately describe. There is no place I would rather be than with the two of you.

Acknowledgments

I would like to first acknowledge both of my parents, Dan and Dee Colucci. I was blessed with wonderful parents whose joint aim in life was to provide a better life for their children. Their love, honesty, strength, and perseverance was—and is— an inspiration to me. Even though as I write this I'm in my 50s, I still try to live every single day in a way that will make them proud.

I had the unique experience of sharing a bedroom with my brother, Dino, for the first 15 years of my life and then being in business with him for the past 21 years. It's a privilege to share that much of your life with a person whom you love and admire. He's the type of person who when you ask, *Can you do me a favor?* always says yes before he ever knows what the favor is. To Dino it doesn't matter. The answer is yes because if you need something . . . anything . . . he's there for you.

My sister, Danielle, is without a doubt one of the nicest people I've ever met. She's one of those people that you love to be around. Always in a good mood, funny, energetic, and talented. If there were more Danielles in the world, we would all benefit.

Lisa Akoury-Ross, Kathleen Tracy, and Lorna Colucci have each provided invaluable support, insight, and guidance in making this book a reality. Also, Howard Johnson for his creative cover and interior layout designs. I am grateful for all that you've brought to the project.

I would also like to acknowledge some of the very good friends I've had the privilege of spending time with throughout the years: Chuck Delagrange, Matt Marcus, Brian Lee, Victor Faragalli, Paul Flavin, John Lamonica, Terry Lamonica, Vinny Eruzione, Diane Kelley, Charlotte Glinka, Kerri Choi, Colleen McCormick, Eddy Pisano, Alison Cayer, Tom DiPrete, Clinton Sparks, Danny, and Sue Colucci. I appreciate each of you and remain grateful for our enduring friendship.

Lastly, I would like to give a shout-out to my hometown of Pompton Lakes, New Jersey; there simply was no better place on earth to grow up. And only people who graduated from PLHS fully understand what it means to have Cardinal pride.

Table of Contents

Introduction

When I was in high school, I had absolutely no idea what I wanted to do for a living or what I wanted out of life. Everyone told me I had plenty of time to figure it out; that's what college was for. So I just waited for something to come to me.

I have plenty of time, I thought. *I'm young.*

Then I blinked and 15 years had passed. Although I had graduated, was employed, and did achieve some advancement, I still lacked a goal, a plan, or any real idea of how to become truly successful—or happy for that matter. Everyone else in my life seemed pleased with where I was professionally, which is to say my parents were thrilled with where I was in life, and my wife was happy that we were able to afford a modest home. But I didn't feel like I had achieved real success at all.

To me, being employed, having the ability to pay my bills, and merely staying afloat was not *success.* And it certainly wasn't fulfilling. So I asked myself two questions: *How did I wind up where I am?* and *How do I change it?*

You see, they teach virtually everything in schools except how to be successful and how to be happy. This book is a practical guide—a roadmap to those two destinations, if you will. It's a how-to book specifically tailored for young adults who are about to embark on this journey we call life. Success is a choice, one that needs to be made right now. You can lead a life filled with fun, passion, excitement, and riches . . . if you choose to.

The aim of this book is to show you precisely how to get there through a formula that if followed, never fails. I believe that what you'll learn in this little book will be far more valuable than anything you learn in high school or will learn in college for that matter. Not that it replaces formal education, but understanding the concepts in this book will be the linchpin to reaching heights you might have never imagined. All you need is a desire to achieve something great.

People love to say that they have no regrets in life. I find that absolutely ridiculous. Are we to believe that every person has made every right choice throughout their lifetime? I have plenty of regrets, but the biggest one by far is that I didn't learn how to become successful until I was well into my 30s. I really wish someone had explained it to me when I was a teenager. It would have saved me a lot of sleepless nights filled with worry.

I want to help you streamline the learning curve so you can begin living an enviable life sooner rather than later. We're not talking about luck here; you will earn it. This is not a how-to-win-the-lottery book; it's a how-to-win-at-life book so you can be financially secure doing something you find exciting while also positively influencing others.

We'll not only cover how to be successful but also how to deal with the negative mind-set and irrational fears that kill ambition and sabotage most people's dreams. You're going to learn how to spot these limiting beliefs and get rid of them before they start running and ruining your life. And perhaps most importantly, you'll learn the importance of thinking for yourself.

The strategy presented in this book is not new nor a secret. It's been around a very long time and is absolutely available to anyone who cares to learn it. One of the earliest books on success, *Think and Grow Rich,* was written by Napoleon Hill in 1937. His idea was to research success in as scientific a way as possible and reduce it to a formula or set of rules that anyone could follow. He interviewed the best and the brightest of the era, Industrial Age titans such as Andrew Carnegie, Henry Ford, and Thomas Edison, and dozens of other millionaires. Although each succeeded in a different facet of life, each did so utilizing the exact same method. Today, the only thing that's changed are the names of the people using that approach. Now it's Carolyn Rafaelian, Daymond John, Jim Carrey, Sara Blakely—and yours truly.

It doesn't matter whether your interests lie in business, music, writing, or inventing. And it doesn't matter if you're a world famous athlete or building a business out of the public eye. The system works for anyone who chooses to use it. And the very first thing you have to get over is thinking that people who are rich and famous are better than you or have skills that are beyond you. Anyone who uses the principles in this book will be successful in any endeavor they choose.

Others have written books covering this topic, but I found the way many chose to deliver the message off-putting, coming across as either hyperactive, slick salesmen or mystical types who conjure images of gentle breezes and wind chimes. While I may find a great deal of value in what they say, their presentations turn off most young people, who quickly tune them out. So this book is intentionally succinct. The information is stripped of fluff, and the topics are presented in a straightforward manner designed to be both informative and respectful of your time.

In return, all that I ask is that you do yourself a favor and make an honest effort to keep an open mind about the material. Everyone believes in gravity because we experience it every day, but no one can actually *see* gravity; what we see is the effect that gravity has on everything. The same is true with this book; hopefully, it will show you the absolute and certain effect this concept has on everyone that uses it.

Congratulations for having the maturity and ambition to buy a book that I hope changes your life.

A Little about Me

My parents both grew up in poverty; they're too proud to admit that, but it's true. I, on the other hand, grew up middle class because my parents worked hard and were determined to give their family a better life. Early on they preached education and the importance of being a decent person as you go through life. And it worked because my siblings and I did fairly well in school and never got into any real trouble to speak of. I certainly had it better than most; my parents were together, we had a great family unit, and they largely kept any financial problems they were having away from us.

I was fortunate enough to get an athletic scholarship to a good school, which secured an education for me. But once I graduated everything changed. I was lost. I had absolutely no idea what to do with my life. I had a succession of low-paying, dead-end jobs that were as embarrassing to me as they were unfulfilling. I knew I wanted a better life, but I didn't know how to achieve it. I was living in a one-room apartment, and even that was more than I could afford. Every month I would hold back one or two bills because I simply didn't have enough money to pay them all. The next month, I would hold back two different bills in an effort to stay just close enough to current so that no one would hire a collection agency to harass me.

Even though I was able to keep a roof over my head it was a lousy way to live. I was really broke. I was constantly anxious about money and simply didn't see any clear path to a successful future.

One of the jobs I had only paid on the last business day of the month. Without fail, I would run out of money two or three days before I received my next check. There were plenty of days when I skipped lunch and made a concerted effort to conserve whatever gas I had in my car because I had no money. On more than one occasion, I ran tolls on the Massachusetts Turnpike because I didn't even have a quarter. Back then you used to throw the change into a basket attached to the toll booth. I would make believe I had thrown the change in and then beep my horn as if I missed. That's how bad it was.

I knew I had to do something, so I decided to go to law school, and that was by default. I had absolutely no interest in being a lawyer but didn't know what else to do. I was also sick of answering the *What are you going to do with your life?* question. I thought that if I was able to graduate from law school, I would at least stand a chance of getting a job that would pay enough to live a decent life. Looking back at my thought process, it's clear to me I wasn't thinking about success at all; it was more a matter of survival. So I borrowed every cent I could to go to law school. I worked full time during the day and went to law school 6:00–10:00 four nights a week.

I kept up this schedule for three-and-a-half very difficult years. My financial problems only got worse because although I continued to live modestly, I was still living beyond my means. I remember one incident where my car broke down, and I simply could not afford to fix it. I called Visa and asked if I could extend my credit limit, and they denied my request.

Trust me, things are dire when Visa denies you a credit extension.

I had pride though, and I wasn't going to ask anyone for the money. I went to my landlord and he agreed to use my security deposit for that month's rent so I could fix my car. While my car was being fixed I borrowed my brother-in-law's car, which had no license plate and was unregistered. Talk about angst. Every time I saw a police officer I thought for sure I was going to get arrested. Thankfully, I never did.

So when I graduated I felt like I had really earned my degree. Eventually, I got a very good job working at a firm, but I still felt unfulfilled. Even though I was making a decent wage by any standard, I still didn't have any real money. This deeply bothered me, so I set out to learn how to make money, how to be successful, and how to craft a life instead of letting life happen to me.

Now I want to teach that to you. I want to save you the sleepless nights, the worry, and the wondering how other people do it. If you pay attention to what comes next, I guarantee you success.

It All Begins with Your Thoughts

My thoughts create my reality.

—Carolyn Rafaelian, founder of Alex and Ani

There are a great many people who have difficulty thinking for themselves. Teenagers and young adults have the added hurdle of not yet being permitted truly independent thought. Sure, we all need guidance from people who have life experience, and there are plenty of mistakes we can avoid by heeding their advice. Parents, teachers, friends, coaches, instructors . . . they all play vital roles in any young person's upbringing, and they can make significant contributions to their life.

But as a young adult you need to start taking ownership of your future and exploring your thoughts. Don't waste precious time living a life that someone else wants you to lead, no matter how well-intentioned that someone else may be. If you are seeking a meaningful life that is filled with passion, excitement, and success in all its forms, you need to chase what inspires you. You need to wake up every morning excited about what lies ahead that day, which doesn't happen unless you are the one at the helm of your destiny. And nothing will affect the outcome of your life as much as your thoughts.

Your mind is a powerful tool. Your mind can convince you that you are capable of great feats and that the arrival of success is nothing more than a matter of time—or it can convince you that success will never happen for you no matter how hard you try because in your heart of hearts you believe that success is something that other people attain. In either instance you are correct.

Henry Ford famously said: "Whether you think you can or think you can't, you're right."

Success is a choice we make. Let me say that again: success is a choice. Even though this may be difficult to understand, billions of people make the choice every day to be *un*successful. Of course no one says: *Today I have made the irrevocable decision NOT to be successful.* It's much more insidious than that. It is how you feel and think on a daily basis that determines your outcome. So if you feel in your heart that you'll never have money or that you're not smart enough or that you aren't good looking enough, or you aren't whatever enough, those beliefs will doom you to an unfulfilled life marked by failure and disappointment.

Remember, your mind is a powerful tool.

These are limiting beliefs. Remember, your mind is a powerful tool. Through your words and feelings, you can convince yourself—and everyone around you—that you either do, or don't, have what it takes. Whatever we think, good or bad, will ultimately be our reality:

I'll never have a car like that . . . . I'll have one in my driveway someday.

I don't know the first thing about starting my own business . . . . I can learn what's necessary to start a business.

If it wasn't for bad luck, I'd have no luck at all.... Everything works out for me.

I've said: *Everything works out for me*, for my entire life. And everything always has.

It goes right through me when I hear someone running themselves down because I'm thoroughly convinced that they are condemning themselves to a life of failure. There are plenty of people who will try to run you down as you go through life; for God's sake don't help them.

The very first step toward happiness and success is the realization that our thoughts—particularly the ones we say out loud and write down—dictate our destiny. For example, Steph Curry was once a nondescript member of the Davidson University basketball team. He was undersized, not heavily recruited, and not expected to ever be a household name. It was during this period that he took a pen and wrote on his sneaker: *I can do all things*. It is no coincidence that in 2016 he was the NBA's first unanimously selected Most Valuable Player.

Now for any of this to sink in you have to open your mind and start viewing things a little differently. When Steph Curry boldly wrote those words on his sneaker perhaps he was the only one who believed that great things lay ahead for him. He understood though that his thoughts would be his reality. It's that simple a concept and that powerful a tool.

What will you be when you grow up? Almost all of us had to write an essay answering that question at one time or another in grade school. I'll also wager that 99 percent of us put absolutely no real thought into it. Interestingly, research shows that people who are specific about what they will achieve and commit it to writing are far more likely to reach their goal.

Case in Point

A fifth-grader from Michigan got this very assignment, but unlike most of us he was specific and definite about what he would achieve. He wrote, "I'm going to play shortstop for the New York Yankees."

Basically, Derek Jeter encapsulated this entire book in a single sentence. He said exactly what he would accomplish with real specificity. He wrote that he would be a professional athlete, then went on to state the team he would play for and the position he would play. I refer to this approach as *confident clarity.*

Derek Jeter didn't say: *I hope to . . .* or *If things go according to plan . . .* or *In a perfect world . . .*

He didn't equivocate at all. He stated precisely what he would do. Confident clarity is where it all begins. You can start spinning the world in your direction tomorrow if you are willing to definitively declare your intentions.

Without goals true success is impossible.

I can already hear the first question: *What if I don't know what I ultimately want to do?* Well, there is absolutely no getting around it: the work starts right there. Without goals true success is impossible. People with no goals float through life letting events dictate where they will go and what they will be instead of charting their own path toward a destination of their choosing. You cannot let this happen.

Think of it in terms of a trip you intend to take. You set

aside time for the trip, plan your itinerary, buy things you'll need, pack certain clothes, get a hotel reservation, buy a plane ticket, etc. Now contemplate this: everything you did leading up to the moment you take your seat on the plane was predicated on *where you were going.* The destination dictates all. You need to know where you're going before you can determine what you will need to get you there.

There are really only four steps to success and this is step one. You need to take the time to think—really think—about what you want out of life, and the earlier you do this the longer you will have to enjoy the fruits and freedoms that come from great success. But rarely will it be immediately apparent. In fact, billionaire movie director Steven Spielberg once gave a fascinating speech on this subject and offered a really unique and interesting perspective on how your destiny might present itself. Spielberg contended that a dream "doesn't often come at you screaming in your face . . . . Sometimes a dream almost whispers . . . . Very hard to hear."

In other words, you have to really pay attention to what excites you, grabs your attention, and compels your interest. In fact, the idea for this book was something that whispered to me. I spent a significant portion of my adult life as a college football coach, and on Thursday nights I would hold a meeting with the kids that covered topics such as life, love, money, success, adversity, etc. In short, everything *but* football. This went on every week, season after season, until one day I realized that I enjoyed giving these life lessons even more than coaching. In fact, I enjoyed it more than just about anything in my professional life. It was challenging, fun, and really fulfilling to provide these young men with another perspective on life. Said another way, my calling was whispering to me, but it took a long time to hear it.

Unless you already know exactly what you want to do with your life, you need to begin your search. Start with whatever you view as ultimate success: accomplishment? fortune? fame? Really think about what type of life's pursuit would bring out your passion and make you the happiest. And if it doesn't come to you instantly, that's okay; but you need to think.

Don't allow yourself to just drift through life waiting for something to grab your attention. Think about what you want to do. Visualize those options and find your passion. And make no mistake about it; you do not need to be a world class athlete to engage this process. Anyone can do it. Sara Blakely proves this point perfectly. And as you read this just know that she's a self-made billionaire who has more than ten times Derek Jeter's net worth.

Case in Point

Sara Blakely graduated from Florida State University and took the LSAT (law school admissions test) because her father was a lawyer, and she wanted to follow in his footsteps. She failed the test—twice. This led to her applying for a job as Goofy at Disney World. But she was rejected because she wasn't tall enough; apparently you have to be at least five foot eight to qualify to be Goofy. At any rate, she eventually landed a job selling fax machines door-to-door. So with a positive attitude and a strong desire to succeed she actually made quite a name for herself as a salesperson, ultimately landing a promotion as a regional sales manager. She was doing well but she wasn't happy.

One night while Sara was preparing to go out she put on pantyhose underneath her pants because she liked how it removed any panty lines. But she hated how her nylon-clad feet looked with open-toe shoes. So she cut the feet off of the pantyhose, and the idea for Spanx was born. But as Sara explained in an interview some years later, the idea was actually born years before.

"The reason I believe I took the idea and ran with it was because of all the advance work [in-depth visualization] I had done. So I said: *OK, I want to invent or create a product that I can sell that's my own and not somebody else's, and I want it to be something I can sell to millions of people. And I want it to be something that makes people feel good.*"

Blakely actually wrote that in a journal that she kept at the time. After committing it to paper she claimed to be on high alert, constantly looking for when it was going to show up in her life.

She added, "The day I cut the feet out of my pantyhose I immediately started pursuing it."

This book is for people with ambition. The doers. And I'm here to tell you exactly what to do to get started. You need to arrive at your goal first and put it in writing just like Derek Jeter and Sara Blakely. Even though it takes incredible courage to share our dreams with others—because we fear being ridiculed—that courage is actually secondary in importance to the discipline of transferring your goals to writing. When you commit a goal to writing, it's like entering into a contract with yourself. There is something about putting it down on paper that propels you forward to achieving whatever your goal may be. You embed in your mind what you want most.

This confident clarity is the groundwork for your success.

Let me give you an example from my own life. I once read that a legendary college football coach maintained a list entitled *100 Things I'll Do Before I Die*. I had read about his philosophy on writing down goals and given his immense success, I decided to try it. I only wanted to write down 25 goals I wanted accomplish before I departed this earth, but I was hard-pressed to come up with even that many. It took me days to finalize my list, but I ultimately did. So with my 25 goals written down, I signed it, dated it, and endeavored to review it once a week until I completed each and every item on the list, no matter how long it took.

Now here is the amazing part: I completed the entire list in two years.

There are several things you should take away from this anecdote. The first is that putting my desires into writing made it somehow prominent in my mind; so much so that I became ever mindful of arranging my life in a way that would allow me to cross off one goal after another, which included:

- ✦ visiting Key West
- ✦ coaching a college football team
- ✦ starting my own business
- ✦ amassing $50,000 in my checking account
- ✦ writing a book

I'm not kidding; I did all of those things plus 20 more in the span of two years. Which brings me to the second thing that should strike you: my goals were too small. I had my own set of limiting beliefs that I wasn't even aware of. I honestly thought it would take me a lifetime to complete that list, a fact that now embarrasses me.

Here's an even better example of how powerful confident clarity is when you combine it with the absolute belief that you will achieve your goals and create your own destiny:

Case in Point

Jim Carrey was 19 when he moved to Hollywood, initially to pursue a career as a standup comic and later as a film actor. In 1985, a broke and depressed Carrey drove his beat-up Toyota up into the Hollywood Hills and parked on Mulholland Drive. While overlooking Los Angeles he daydreamed of success. He visualized having conversations with directors he respected and having his name on the marquee of movie theaters. He said it made him feel better.

One night in 1990, Carrey wrote himself a check for $10 million for *acting services rendered*, postdated to Thanksgiving Day 1995. He kept the folded check in his wallet and would take it out from time to time. He believed—and specifically declared—what his goal was and wrote down a date when he would attain it.

Over the next five years he earned millions for movies like *Ace Ventura: Pet Detective.* Not long before Thanksgiving 1995 New Line Cinema cast Carrey in *Dumb and Dumber.* His salary *for acting services rendered* was $10 million.

Now you can think him crazy for having these imaginary conversations and dreaming of his name on the marquee, but I see it as an awesome example of how confident clarity never fails.

Throughout this book I'll try to anticipate your questions and concerns. At this point, I imagine many of you thinking: *It simply can't be that easy.* My response to that is: *You're right.* As Carrey noted, visualization had to be coupled with hard work. "You can't just visualize and then go have a sandwich and wait for it to happen."

Carrey believed he would be a great success, but he combined it with a plan. So you see, it all starts with confident clarity. That clear goal is written down and read daily, embedding in your mind what you will attain.

Think of it this way: I want you to start at the finish line. *You* have to decide what your particular success will look like. It's a mistake trying to attain another person's concept of success. It has to be what you desire most. And if your definition and/or vision of success differs from what your friends and family want for you, so be it.

The first step in taking ownership of your future starts here.

The Takeaway

✔ Success is a choice. And the formula to success has only four steps. Everything that follows in this book relates to one of these four steps.

   1. Put in honest hard work to determine your life's goal and write it down.

   2. Recognize and overcome the fears that are holding you back.

3. Visualize it as if it's already happened.

4. Relentlessly pursue your dream.

✔ Follow these four steps, and I guarantee you not only phenomenal success, but true happiness and contentment. Money without contentment is really just well-dressed failure.

TASK: At the end of every chapter I'm going to ask you to make an investment in your future by successfully completing a task. Right now I want you getting to work thinking long and hard about what you want out of life. Before you read any further, write down three goals. You can put them in your phone, on your tablet, or jot them down on a piece of paper you can carry in your phone case (which is what I do).

Do not take any shortcuts—write down three goals before moving on.

Don't Let Fear Get in Your Way

Fear kills more dreams than failure ever will.

—Suzy Kassem

Once you've arrived at a goal based on some deep thought and soul searching, you're ready to move on to recognizing and overcoming limiting beliefs. This might be your single biggest obstacle toward reaching your goals. Only a chosen few are born with a sense that they will conquer the world because they choose to. The vast majority of people struggle with some set of limiting beliefs, so the sooner you can identify this problem in your own life, the sooner you can overcome it on your way to an enviable, rich, and noteworthy life.

There are two kinds of limiting beliefs, the first of which is self-imposed.

At the root of all self-imposed limiting beliefs, whether we want to admit it or not, is fear. I detest the concept of fear. Oh, it's often disguised as practicality, caution, patience, bad luck, misfortune, selflessness, bad timing, and a whole host of other excuses. But it's always fear. So then the question begs: what the hell are we all so afraid of?

I think Mark Twain showed incredible insight when he said

that 99 percent of the things he spent a lifetime worrying about never actually happened. That is absolutely true, which means we waste 99 percent of our time when we worry. Successful people still experience fear from time to time; they just don't give into it. They prefer to look at a particular situation as one of managed risk, as opposed to unfounded fear.

Robert Kiasaki, author of the tremendous book *Rich Dad, Poor Dad*, came up with a great mnemonic: FEAR stands for *false events appearing real.* There are always reasons, which you can convince yourself are absolutely valid, not to pursue your dreams. *I'm too old. I'm too young. I don't have the money. I don't have the experience. It's not the right time. I don't have the time. I missed my window. I didn't get a good enough education. I can't go back to school at my age. I'm too set in my ways. I'm too different. I have a handicap. I'm not good with money. I'm not detail oriented. I get bored too easily. I'm not cut out to make it big. It's my parents' fault.*

FEAR stands for false events appearing real.

Blah, blah, blah, blah.

And it only gets worse when you get older. Take all these excuses, add a million more, shake it all up, and you have one huge pile of fear.

From this point forward you need to be honest with yourself. Recognize fear and limiting beliefs as nothing more than obstacles you need to go around. I speak from experience when I say there's always a way to get things done. And I do mean *always*. This is absolutely key in going from stop to start, poor to rich, unhealthy to fit, or good to great. It doesn't matter how big or small your dream is. Fear will be there just waiting to bully you into stopping. Don't give in.

Limiting beliefs can follow you around like a perpetual

dark cloud. And when it's self-imposed, people often have no trouble verbalizing it: *Every day just goes from bad to worse . . . You need to have money to make money, so I guess I'm never going to have any.* (I can't tell you how much I hate even writing that.) Whatever you say will come true. It is that simple. Whether you think you can or can't—you're right. So think you can!

I have one friend who routinely took the concept of self-defeating talk to another level. Below is an actual, verbatim exchange we once had:

Me: "Would you like to try fly fishing?"

Him: "No! That's stupid."

Me: "Why is that stupid?"

Him: "Because it is. I don't know how to fly fish. I'm uncoordinated, and I'll probably wind up gettin' a hook caught in my eye, and I'll be blind for life. Not interested. Forget it."

Instead of calling him out as being a slave to his limiting beliefs and how they were not only running but ruining his life, I decided to try and reform him. The next day, completely undaunted by his negativism, I brought a fly rod and reel to where he was and told him I was going to teach him how to cast. After some cajoling he relented and quickly realized that it was easier than he thought. In other words, I demystified the whole process and took the fear out of him one backcast at a time. I watched as trepidation gave way to a little smile.

Once he overcame his limiting beliefs and fears, a whole new and exciting world opened up for him. As a matter of fact, fly fishing has become his single greatest passion. I've never seen anyone get more pure joy out of the sport than him. He and I have traveled far and wide, from the exotic to the familiar, in search of great fishing and adventure: Alaska, Montana, Cape Cod, the Catskills, Islamorada, the Baja Peninsula, and Belize. Consider all he would have missed had he not moved past his self-imposed limiting belief. The void it would have left in his life is incalculable.

After you recognize your limiting beliefs, you need to get to work on eradicating them. One tried and true method is through the use of affirmations. An affirmation is a mantra, or phrase, that you repeat to yourself over and over again. The actual wording has to be entirely yours and based on what you want to attain.

Let's say your desire is to graduate first in your class in high school. But you're afraid in the end you might just fall short. You need to fix in your mind that you *will* be the valedictorian of the class. Picture yourself at the lectern giving the commencement address. Visualize all the people in the audience and exactly what kind of day it is. Imagine your parents and relatives smiling back at you, proud of your accomplishments. I'd even start writing my speech. Visualize it every night. Put yourself to sleep thinking about it, all the while repeating your affirmation: *I will be the valedictorian of the class.*

Even if you are the type of person who naturally lacks confidence, somehow you will eventually begin to believe it. And that belief will guide your subconscious choices as well as your conscious ones and lead you exactly where you want to be.

I know what you're thinking: again, it can't be that easy.

Listen, I didn't invent this concept; it's been around since the Bible. *Act as if ye had faith and faith will be given to you.* I'm just bringing the concept into the present day. This is something I've done for decades and have benefitted from it in more ways than I can express. I don't say that to impress you, but rather to impress upon you how effective affirmations are.

Act as if ye had faith and faith will be given to you.

My current affirmation—and I've had many—is:

> I am and will remain grateful for all that
> I have in my life. I will become a highly
> successful author, writing a book that never
> goes out of print and positively affects
> young people on a mass scale. I will use
> the book as a springboard to a speaking
> career aimed at getting people to adopt
> this way of thinking. I will continue to be
> a magnet for money and opportunity. All of
> these goals will be attained and positively
> affect my relationships with friends,
> family, and most especially my wife.

I repeat this affirmation every morning on my way to work and truly believe that it will absolutely happen.

Now I want to be 100 percent honest in writing this book, so I admit that I'm not immune to doubt. But when doubt creeps in now and again, I remind myself that doubt will only work to hinder me from attaining my goals. And at that moment, I always repeat the above mantra to remind myself of what I will accomplish.

If confidence does not come naturally to you, this is a way to begin to manufacture it. So don't wait; write out your own affirmation before you go to bed tonight. And if you have not yet arrived at your goal, keep thinking about it. Don't leave it to fate! You'll be very sorry if you do.

For as debilitating as self-imposed limiting beliefs are, far more people suffer from the second form of limiting beliefs, those that are foisted upon them by others trying to convince them that they can't do something. What a terrible sin to make someone else feel inferior or deficient. I would add that it's a bigger sin to allow someone to make you question your self-worth, but to a degree it's human nature. When someone tells another that they aren't smart, or pretty, or qualified, or (fill in the blank), we tend to believe them. Though you have to ask yourself why you would let another person define who and what you are, or who and what you can be. I've always been particularly intrigued by people who heard the harsh criticism and persevered nonetheless. Nothing demonstrates this point better than the story of Walmart founder Sam Walton.

Case in Point

Walmart is arguably the most revolutionary and profitable retail store there has ever been. In his 20s, Sam worked for J.C. Penney. I don't just mean the store; I mean that he worked for Mr. J.C. Penney. After some time had passed, Mr. Penney called in young Sam and told him that he wasn't cut out for retail.

Now, this particular piece of criticism was coming from a then-titan of the retail world. You have to imagine that someone as successful, accomplished, and rich as Penney would know who was and was not cut out for retail, wouldn't you? The answer is NO. If you believe in yourself—a feeling that you will develop after reading this book—nothing should deter you from your objectives. Nothing.

Sam Walton certainly wasn't deterred. He walked out, gathered himself, licked his wounds, and started his own retail shop, which would eventually spawn an empire and far outdistanced anything that JCPenney ever did, all because he refused to let someone else's opinion define him.

You have to know and accept that success never comes to people who procrastinate, give up, or are dissuaded by the naysayers. If you determine that someone has a valid criticism, by all means take it into account and make necessary adjustments, but for God's sake don't quit.

Please know that I'm not instructing you to do anything that I haven't already done. I have long made a practice of reading a story like Sam Walton's, remembering it, and then applying the lesson in my own life when a similar situation arises. Let me give you a concrete example of how a book like this can positively affect your entire life in the same way that Sam Walton's story affected mine.

When I graduated from law school, I was offered a job with one of the most prestigious law firms in Boston. It was a small firm, maybe 12 lawyers, but simply one of the best in the field of tort law. I worked hard, applied myself, and enjoyed some early success. I even became friends with the managing partner, a 63-year-old legal legend who was admired by all. I was, at times, the envy of the other associates when the big boss would ask me if I was free on a particular weekend to go fishing on his boat.

I had been at the firm for two and a half years and was confident that I was doing well. Then came my review. For reasons that I don't understand to this day, I was let go. Fired. Terminated. Even worse than that, the big boss—my friend and fishing buddy—told me that it was the collective wisdom of the partnership that I was not cut out for tort law. To make matters worse, he added that he was telling me that out of friendship.

Now you have to consider the source: It was not some knucklehead uncle fond of crushing beer cans on his forehead at parties telling me this; it was coming from an accomplished man who I really respected.

So there I was, fired by my friend and mentor, told that I

wasn't good enough to succeed in the field, and about one month away from an inability to pay my bills. Did I feel fear? Absolutely. I not only felt fear but anger, amazement, disillusionment, and despair. However, I remembered Sam Walton. I imagined that he must have felt the same way. I'm sure he wondered if his mentor was right and whether or not he should try a different profession. But ultimately he said no to all of that noise, and so did I.

Two weeks later, I opened my own law firm, practicing strictly in tort law, and it was the best and most lucrative decision of my life. I've owned the firm for 20 years now. I've enjoyed complete autonomy, made millions of dollars, employed dozens of people, and helped thousands of clients, all because I paid attention to the story of Sam Walton and believed in myself.

Let me give you one more example.

Case in Point

A teenager in North Carolina had dreams of playing professional basketball. He tried out for his high school team as a sophomore knowing that it was the first step toward securing a college scholarship and ultimately achieving stardom at the professional level. But the coach didn't see it that way. The teen was cut after tryouts.

Like most young adults faced with disappointment, fear (false events appearing real) immediately consumed him. *Now I'll never get a scholarship. I won't be a collegiate basketball star, and I'll never be an NBA player.* But instead of giving into his spiraling fears he went to see the coach and asked what he could do to improve as a player so that he could have a better chance of making the team as a junior. The coach explained what parts of his game were deficient and then made him an offer: he would be willing to give the teen one-on-one instruction for an hour every day. The catch was that he'd have to come in before school started.

The young man certainly didn't relish getting up early every day, but he believed in himself and his dreams and decided to put in the work. So he agreed and never missed a single morning workout. Not only did Michael Jordan make the team the following season, but he went on to an amazing career at the University of North Carolina en route to one of the greatest pro careers in history. His global fame then gave him entrée into a sneaker and fashion empire worth billions, all because he refused to let someone else's opinion deter him from his goals.

————————————————

Now there certainly is such a thing as constructive criticism, which can be enormously helpful. So I'm not saying that you should dismiss any and all criticism. If you determine that the criticism is valid, don't quit; make the necessary adjustments. That's just smart. But how do you handle criticism you believe to be unfounded, even if it is from someone you respect? Well, it takes guts. It's not easy to persevere when you have the misfortune to be around naysayers. You have to find it in yourself to say: *They're wrong*, or *I'll prove them wrong*, and press on. (To my knowledge, there has never been a statue erected of a critic.)

If on the other hand, you are faced with criticism from someone you don't respect, ignore it. To do anything else is silly.

The Takeaway

- ✔ If in your heart of hearts you can't muster the confidence to believe, you're going to struggle and really inhibit your ability to succeed.
- ✔ Affirmations are a way to convince yourself that your destiny is preordained. Use them daily.
- ✔ Recognize any limiting beliefs that are holding you back.
- ✔ Recognize that limiting beliefs, regardless of whether they are self-imposed or foisted upon you, are nothing more than obstacles you need to go around.
- ✔ Don't let fear or criticism stop you.

TASK: Reread the goals you wrote down at the end of Chapter 1. Believe each one will happen. Then create an affirmation that incorporates only the goals that you will achieve and the areas of your life that you will improve. Again write it in your phone, tablet, or on paper—any place that's convenient and allows you to view your affirmation whenever you want to.

Always Ask for Advice

No enemy is worse than bad advice.

—Sophocles

As you set out on your path to success there will be times, particularly at the beginning, when you feel like you are in need of direction. *Should I go to college? What should I major in? Do I start my own business? Should I accept this job offer? Should I go to graduate school? Should I invest in that piece of real estate,* etc.

In most circumstances we turn to those who love us for the answers: parents, friends, and family. It goes without saying that they are well-intentioned and we trust them, but are they qualified to dispense advice on the particular subject at issue? This is a question that's rarely ever asked.

When I was a young man, my father was a dominant force in my life. He was smart, willful, persuasive, and certain that he knew what was best for me. And to be fair, he usually *did* know what was best and for the most part doled out great advice. But there were times I disagreed with what he was telling me, and to make matters even more difficult, he would often come on so strongly in defense of his position that I simply could not make my own decision for fear of insulting him.

This situation dogged me for decades. It was done out of love, but I eventually realized that nearly all of his advice was based on wanting me to do the safest thing possible. It makes perfect sense if you really think about it: a parent's primary job is to keep their children safe. But the safest path is not necessarily the right path.

The safest path is not necessarily the right path.

In a nutshell, he wanted me to get a good education from a good school, get a good job with a good pension, and buy a house as soon as I was able. So what does one study in order to get a good education? What would I be doing at my good job? And would my good pension be enough for me to live the life I desired in retirement? Again, I love my father and appreciate that he cared so much about me to take the time to offer the very best advice he had, but in reality his advice didn't constitute any plan at all. It also presupposed that I would work for someone else for my whole career, earn what that person or company was willing to pay me, and be dependent on a pension that someone else arranged. His advice did not take into account what I wanted to do with my life or what I wished to work toward.

If a teenager asks their parent: *Where do you think I should go to college?* I would imagine that the best response would be: *Well, that depends; what do you want to do with your life?* Going to the very best agricultural school would be a four-year waste of time if your desire was to be a film maker.

Every moment of your life should count. If ever you find yourself wishing time away, you're in the wrong situation. I actually have friends who have said out loud: *I just have to get through 18 more years, and then I'm onto retirement.* How does that make sense? You're going to suffer through a job you hate and wish away the passage of time—often 30 years or so—just so you can retire with a pension?

I can't help but think that if you are crossing off days on a calendar trying to reach a retirement date that's years away, you are wasting the only life you have to work with. In effect, these people are choosing to count their days instead of making their days count. I'll bet that most people who find themselves in that position wound up there not by choice but by inertia. When you question these same people, as I have, about the choices that put them there, they invariably say it sort of just happened.

You need to take responsibility for your own life, your own path, and your own future.

But let's get back to advice. You need to take responsibility for your own life, your own path, and your own future. Take charge by putting in the time to decide where your passions lie, research who succeeded in the field of your choosing, and then actually seek out someone who can give you the benefit of their experience reaching the success you now seek. Believe it or not, many highly successful people will be more than happy to answer your questions either in person, over the phone, or through email. They can tell you the best and worst decisions they ever made; help you avoid pitfalls; give you tips to expedite your growth; and perhaps even suggest a detailed plan to follow.

Rich people, by and large, are among the most generous individuals you'll ever find. And when I say generous I mean with their time as well as their money. They welcome the opportunity to mentor young, aggressive success seekers and take real pride in helping them reach their goals.

Carolyn Rafaelian, the creator of the jewelry company Alex and Ani and one of *Forbes* magazine's richest women in

America, expresses her desire to help others achieve success as a core principle of her business. She's actually created a division of her company that she calls the Alex and Ani Institute whose stated objective is to "share the secret of our success and energy to help others attain their goals." Although Carolyn is a shining example of the largess of successful people, she is more the rule than the exception. Successful people by and large will help you, but the onus is on you to either straight out ask for their help, or seek out information about them that you can use as a GPS of sorts.

Asking for advice or help shouldn't carry the stigma that it does. I can't think of a smarter thing to do than ask for advice about how to become successful from a successful person. So if you have the gumption and see the value in this approach, there are several strategies you can use. Research to identify the best person to contact. You can use networking connections to find someone who knows the person or an appropriate means to contact them—with the advent of social media, it's never been easier. You can pretty much leave a message on virtually anyone's Facebook page or get their email address if you do a little digging. Don't forget that a successful person is not necessarily famous. They might very well be flattered that you are even asking for their help and/or guidance and consequently, eager to offer it.

Whether you attempt to contact them by email or actually get a meeting, please be prepared. Do research on the person so you know as much about them as possible. Again, the person will find it flattering, but even more importantly it should help you formulate pertinent questions. *Why did you leave your first job? How did you find out about that particular piece of property that you purchased? How did you capitalize on the proceeds of that deal? Do you feel that graduating from Dartmouth was extremely helpful and if so, in what way? What was the turning point in your career that allowed you to get to the position you enjoy today? What role did mentors play in your rise through the company? What did you do to seek out the right mentors? What was your biggest mistake along the way to success?* And so on.

The more initiative you demonstrate in your preparation, the more forthcoming the person will be. It won't be enough that you are there; you have to demonstrate that you are willing to walk the walk by showing some diligence and industriousness before the meeting ever takes place. If you impress them enough you might even wind up with a mentor who wants to play a part in your rise to the top.

Be courteous in all your dealings with people, but especially when asking for someone's time. Think about what you're going to say before you actually approach the person. In other words, craft how you are going to phrase your request. Courtesy is a lost art, but I really can't overstate its importance.

> *I would really love the opportunity to speak with you for 15 or 30 minutes as your schedule allows.*
>
> *I know you're very busy, but if you could ever find 15 or 30 minutes to talk I would really appreciate it.*
>
> *I would make myself available around your schedule, of course, if there was any way we can actually meet to discuss this.*

And if the person responds: *The only time I can meet is 5:00 a.m. on a Saturday*, your answer should be: *Perfect, I'll be there. Thank you very much. I really appreciate you making time for me like that.*

When someone picks an odd time for a meeting, it's a test. In other words, how badly do you want success? Show your resolve without hesitation. Be enthusiastic and be grateful.

You'll score points immediately. You are the one that stands to gain from this meeting so getting up early is a very small price to pay. The rest is common sense: Don't be on time; be early. Dress appropriately. Write your questions down. Don't overstay your welcome. And always remember that no one ever learned anything with their mouth open. (Listen more than you speak.)

Another method that will help your life's pursuit is to learn about successful people through reading, films, podcasts, whatever. I can't tell you how many biographies I've read, programs I've watched, or broadcasts I've listened to in an effort to learn. I want you to pay close attention to this next anecdote because I feel that it encompasses so much of what I'm trying to get across to you.

I was watching the news one night and a person being interviewed referenced a man named Pat Croce, who started out as a team trainer and ended up the owner of the Philadelphia 76ers. For the record, I had never heard of Croce. I'm not from Philadelphia, and although I love sports I'm not particularly interested in basketball. So why would his story appeal to me? Come on . . . a guy who went from taping ankles to owning the team? How could you not want to know how that happened?

I immediately looked up whether anyone had ever written a biography about him and found out that indeed someone had. So I invested twenty-seven dollars and started reading, and it turned out to be some of the best money I ever spent. I learned so many things from his story that I have profited from in so many ways. In an effort to illustrate how to read a biography and truly learn from it I've distilled the story down to 10 lessons learned. As you read this, please remember that success leaves a trail of bread crumbs, and it's up to you to find and apply them in your own endeavors.

Although he had always had an interest in medicine, he didn't think that medical school was for him. So he became a physical therapist.

Lesson 1. *Study an area of real interest to you and work hard.*

His dream job was to work in professional sports, and more specifically, for a professional sports team in his home town. So he applied for a position with the Philadelphia Eagles. Unfortunately, the team did not see the wisdom in offering young Pat Croce a position. Although disheartened by the rejection, he remained undaunted. He then applied for and got a job with the Philadelphia 76ers as their trainer.

Lesson 2. *Don't be deterred by rejection; keep after your dreams.*

He had fulfilled a dream and loved his job, but after years of work he became restless. Even the attainment of a dream isn't necessarily the end of the road. You have to listen to yourself and trust what you hear. Pat trusted what he heard and started looking for a new challenge. Despite having landed a plum job, he kept his mind open to other possible ventures and opportunities.

You control your destiny.

Lesson 3. *You control your destiny. Don't just let things happen to you and accept whatever comes. Be open to improving your situation.*

Croce made friends wherever he went and did it by being nice to everyone he came in contact with; his goal was to collect friends and never lose one no matter what. He made it his business to know the owner, the players, the coaches, and the janitors.

Lesson 4. *Treat everyone with respect and courtesy regardless of their position. It always pays off—for them and you.*

As Croce spent more time thinking about money and picturing a new future, he began to see different possibilities and potential avenues for advancement.

Lesson 5. *The more you keep something in the forefront of your mind, the greater chance you have of attracting what you want.*

Croce ultimately had the idea of starting his own physical therapy practice within a local hospital. At the time no one had ever done that in Philadelphia. He was energized, did his homework, and pitched the idea to the powers that be at a local facility. Although hesitant, they agreed.

Lesson 6. *Don't be deterred by being the first to ever do something.*

After several years of hard work, Croce turned the PT department into a money maker for the hospital but not for himself personally. He was making somewhere in the vicinity of $35,000 per year as an employee of the hospital. When he concluded that the administration wasn't rewarding him for his success, he decided it was time to open his own practice. But when he told the hospital management of his plans, they panicked. They didn't want to lose him and offered to double his salary. Despite having a wife and a family, he turned down the raise, borrowed $5,000 from his father-in-law, and opened his own facility.

Through hard work, enthusiasm, and some great marketing, he turned his rehabilitation center into a tremendous success. It was so successful that he decided to open another, and another, and another. After being in business for 10 years, Croce had opened 40 PT centers. But just like at the hospital, he grew restless and started contemplating a different future. Like magic, a company soon approached him and offered $40 million for his operation. (See Lesson 5.) He was a multimillionaire.

Lesson 7. *Follow your passion and the money will come.*

Pat Croce knew two things for certain at this point: he was too young to sit around and do nothing, and he did not know what to do with $40 million.

Lesson 8. *Money doesn't make you smarter.*

He knew that he needed advice. The only really rich person he knew was his old boss, the owner of the Philadelphia 76ers. So Croce called and asked if he could meet him for lunch to discuss this issue. The owner of the team was flattered and agreed to the meeting.

Lesson 9. *Ask advice from people who are in the best position to give advice on a particular subject.*

At their meeting, Croce listened to his old boss complain about the team, about the players, the fans, the league, and so on. Although Croce had gone there for advice, he kept his ears open and began to see a vision of his future.

"Sell the team to me," he blurted out.

His old boss chuckled a little and said, "I'm afraid that $40 million isn't nearly enough to buy a professional basketball team."

Croce later said that he left that lunch exhilarated because the owner never said no.

Lesson 10. *Don't hear no when it comes to your dreams.*

It's not enough that you learn the above lessons; you have to start reading articles and books and learn how to absorb the stories and then recall the principles when you're faced with important decisions. I want to illustrate this point with an anecdote from my own life where I applied the *never hear no* principle I first learned from Pat Croce.

When I read Croce's biography, I was a partner in a small firm. I decided that we needed to buy our own building instead of continuing to pay rent. I found a building that was perfect. It had enough room for the firm as then constituted, provided room for expansion, and even offered additional space for us to rent out offices. It was ideal.

One of my partners knew the owner so I asked him to approach the gentleman to see if he was interested in selling. My partner said we'd be wasting our time. He wouldn't sell. But I believed that we would own that building, and I was determined to get it. I told him to ask anyway. Reluctantly, he called and spoke to the owner.

My partner came back with an *I told you so* expression and said that the owner wasn't interested in selling.

"Tell me exactly what he said."

"He said that he didn't see this as the right time to sell."

I immediately smiled. "He didn't say no."

My partner heard no, but I didn't because I read Croce's book. I told my partner to wait two weeks and ask him again. At first he actually refused, repeating that it was a waste of time, but I persisted. Two weeks later the same thing happened. The owner said that he couldn't see how it could work for him at that particular time.

Again, I didn't hear no. But I did think about what he said: *I don't see how it could work for me.* What did that mean? *If there's an obstacle here how can I get around it?* And then I thought: *I wonder if he would sell the building off in pieces as office condominiums?*

I convinced my partner to try again and had him approach the man with my suggestion. About an hour later my partner returned with a bewildered look on his face.

"He thought about it for 10 seconds and said: *Now that will work for me.*"

Our firm is in that space to this day. We've made hundreds of thousands of dollars in rent and have equity now in a piece of property that comprises a part of our retirement planning. All because I learned not to hear no. I tell you this to impress upon you the importance of taking these concepts, learning them, retaining them, and then utilizing them when opportunities present themselves.

The Takeaway

- ✔ Only seek advice from the right people.
- ✔ Try to find people who have succeeded in the area of your interest.
- ✔ Whenever learning about how someone became successful, make certain to apply the lessons learned to your life.

TASK: Identify one person, famous or not, who has succeeded in your area of interest.

4

Take Action

Hope is not a plan

—Anderson Cooper

As previously explained, nothing is more important to achieving success than believing you will. Therein lies the secret sauce of success. However, belief without action is hope, and hope is not a plan. I once heard a priest tell a joke that illustrates my point perfectly.

Belief without action is hope, and hope is not a plan.

Louie was sitting alone in church and began praying to God about something he wanted so badly. *Lord, I've been a good man all my life. I've been true to my wife, I've taken care of my family, and I never miss church. I would like to ask you for just one thing: can I please win the lottery. You say ask and ye shall receive, so I'm asking. Please let me win the lottery.*

He didn't.

The next week Louie returned to church. He purposely waited for everyone to leave so he could again speak directly to God. *I don't understand. I truly believed that if I came to you as a man and asked for something that I really wanted, that you would give it to me. After all, I've led the kind of life that should please you. So I'll ask again, with all due respect, please just let me win the lottery.*

He didn't.

The following week Louie returned to church for one last chat with God. *I'm really disappointed that you wouldn't give me the only thing that I ever asked for. Why are you turning your back on my request when I truly, in my heart, believed that you would grant me this wish?*

Suddenly, the church shook and Louie heard the booming voice of God. *"Louie!"*

Immediately Louie dropped to his knees. "Yes, God?"

"Meet me halfway; buy a ticket!"

I never said it was a great joke, but it perfectly demonstrates the point. Believing that something will happen is essential, but things will move along so much quicker if you take even minimal action toward making your dreams come true. But why do people have such a tough time beginning anything? Why are the first steps often the hardest to take? The answer of course is fear.

Remember earlier when I wrote that you should start at the end? That's precisely what these people do, except they assume that they will fail so why ever try? These same people would rather, in essence, never begin to pursue a dream for fear that it will ultimately end in disappointment. They would rather keep alive the fantasy of success as opposed to dealing with the possibility of failure. Let's really break down this mentality because it's clear to me that so many people fall into this unfortunate category.

Fear remains that constant, insidious cancer that lurks in most people. You have to be able to identify it when it starts to adversely affect you. So let's take as an example a person who has the dream to be an author. If you are that person, then you need to sit down and write something. Anything. Pick a subject and write. Write an article as if it was going into a magazine. Write a description of something you saw that day. Write about the fact that you want to be a writer. It doesn't matter what you write about because in this process you will be:

- ✦ overcoming a fear
- ✦ proving to yourself that you can do it
- ✦ keeping your goal fixed in your mind as you'll be actively working toward its attainment
- ✦ beginning to create forward momentum

One of the best stories to illustrate what we've talked about thus far is that of author Stephen King, one of the most successful authors in the past 50 years. He has sold more than three hundred million books and many have been made into movies. But his story is even more interesting.

Case in Point

Stephen grew up in abject poverty, but he had one thing going for him: he knew exactly what he wanted to do with his life and was committed to it. Even as a boy he began writing stories and submitting them to magazines, and in each instance he would receive a form letter rejecting his submission. But unlike many of us, he persevered and was completely undaunted. Thanks to his mind-set he never got discouraged. In fact, he pinned the rejection letters to his wall. He said that at one point he got so many of them that he needed to replace the thumbtack with a spike.

Then the turning point came. Stephen received a handwritten rejection letter and was thrilled that it wasn't a form letter. Rather than focus on the rejection, he saw it as significant progress, and it emboldened him to keep writing. The rest of this story from my perspective is absolutely predictable. He eventually wrote something that became a tremendous success and started him on a literary career that positively affected tens of millions of people and brought him incredible fame, fortune, and fulfillment.

In essence, that whole story embodies this book. You should also consider, just in case you are still doubting yourself, that Stephen King did not grow up with money, affluence, connections, or go to an Ivy League school. He grew up in circumstances that were probably not as fortunate as yours, yet he became an international success.

Now let me give you an example from my own experience; since I am not Stephen King, perhaps you will be able to identify with this more easily. When I decided to try my hand at writing, I had no idea how to begin, and I had every fear that you would expect from a first-time author. *What if I get writer's block? I've never really written anything before. I don't have an outline. I don't have a fully formed story. What if what I write is boring?*

Fear . . . fear . . . fear . . . fear.

But I eventually recognized these thoughts as fear and decided that I wouldn't give into it. I had a germ of an idea for a book, so I sat down at a computer and told myself that I would write one page. Good or bad, right or wrong, well-crafted, or discombobulated—it didn't matter. I was going to write one page.

As I did, one page turned into two pages, which gave way to Chapter 1, which became the first 100 pages. Seven months later, I had written an entire book. And much to my amazement somewhere along the way I had stopped fearing it and began to get excited about the idea of writing. I found out I had a talent I hadn't been aware of. All because I acknowledged the fear that I had, refused to give into it, and wrote one page.

Once I wrote *The End* I kept thinking of and relying on the story of Stephen King. That helped me get over the angst associated with submitting a manuscript to a publisher for their consideration. It also helped me deal with every rejection letter I got. I no longer saw it as a disappointment but as a stepping stone toward my success. My mind-set was, and remains, that I will be a highly successful, published author, all because I read the story of Stephen King and applied the principles to my own life.

Let's look at it from another angle. My friend, the same one who became the fly fisherman without blinding himself, apparently hadn't fully accepted the concepts in this book when he called me about a job he was interested in. He told me that a local high school was looking for a head football coach, and it was a job he would love to have.

"Apply," I said.

"No, that's stupid. I'd never get it. I don't have any head coaching experience, and I'd probably choke in the interview if they even gave me one."

I was actually shocked that he was reverting back to his knee-jerk negativism. But I wouldn't let him off the hook. "Apply," I said.

"I don't even have a résumé, and I'm a terrible writer."

"No, no, no," I said. "Go home and write a résumé. At least sit down and write a draft and send it to me. I'll look it over and edit it. Then call me, and we'll practice interview questions."

I think he just needed a push in the right direction. He did write a draft that turned into a résumé that eventually got him an interview. I explained to him that just getting and attending the interview would be very helpful. He would get confidence just having gone through it, and at the minimum it would make him that much better prepared the next time an opportunity arose.

But I added, "None of that will actually matter, though, because you're going to get this job."

He allowed himself to believe that it was possible and started talking in phrases like; *When I get the job . . .* or *The first thing I'm going to do when I take over . . .*

So what happened? He got the job. As a matter of fact, his teams eventually had great success, which helped transform not only the school but the entire community. That's not an exaggeration. I attended a game in which his team was facing a rival school that they hadn't beaten in 14 years. When my friend's team triumphed, half the student body and three dozen parents rushed onto the field. This was a community that, years prior, never had much of a football following at all, let alone people kissing, hugging, crying, and chanting. It was an amazing sight to behold and one that would have never taken place if he had given into his initial fears and never even applied for the job.

In the above example I forced my friend forward. I'm hoping this book will do the same for you. But you have to do your part and buy a ticket. Real success will never come from laziness, blind luck, or a bad attitude. They say that *fortune favors the bold*; well, truer words were never spoken.

Once you've fixed it in your mind that you will attain a certain something, you need to create some forward momentum. And believe me, a good plan today is better than a perfect plan tomorrow.

A good plan today is better than a perfect plan tomorrow.

Remember that out of small beginnings can come incredible successes.

Case in Point

What do Amazon, Apple, Disney, Google, Harley Davidson, Hewlett Packard, Lotus Cars, Mattel, Maglite, and Yankee Candle have in common? They were all started in a garage. To further illustrate the point, Jeff Bezos, the founder of Amazon, walked away from a six-figure job and moved his family across the country to fulfill the dream of creating his own company in the vast and uncharted world of Internet sales. He took action every day in his family's garage starting in 1994 and didn't actually sell his first book until 1995. Twenty years later the company that he founded in the most modest of surroundings is the largest online retailer in the world. According to the *New York Times*, in 2015 Amazon reported $29 billion in revenue.

So you have to believe that it will happen; take action, no matter how small, toward your goal; and see the action you are taking as a necessary step toward your ultimate success.

The Takeaway

✔ Hope is not a plan.

✔ You need to create forward momentum with your actions.

✔ Recognize how fear is holding you back in big and small ways.

✔ Replace fear with action.

TASK: Take an affirmative step toward the attainment of your dream by doing *something*. If you want to be an author, write a short story; if you want to be an artist, buy a brush and some paint; if you want to be the CEO of a Fortune 500 company, read a biography of someone who has already attained that goal.

5

Invest in Your Goals

An inch of movement will bring you closer
to your goals than a mile of intention.
—Dr. Steve Maraboli

This next section is critical. How dedicated are you to your desire to be successful? What are you willing to do? Anytime you take action toward your goal, as previously discussed, you move much closer to its attainment. But let's be specific about what you can do to move toward your dreams in leaps and bounds.

Attending seminars, reading books, and watching documentaries about successful people are all great ways to gain knowledge about a particular field or a particular approach someone may have used to achieve success. You are bound to pick up one or two—or 100—kernels of wisdom that you'll benefit from later on. However, it's been my experience that the single most effective way to gain practical experience, to meet the right people, to network, and to further your ambitions is to volunteer. So open up your mind, and let me make my case as to why volunteering is so effective.

Sometimes I feel that people hear the word *volunteer* and

think *charity work*. What I'm talking about is more along the lines of investing in a tried and true avenue that can lead to handsome profits. After all, that's why people invest in the first place: sacrifice now in the hope of creating an abundance for later.

Case in Point

The perfect illustration of this point is the story of Roger Staubach, who was one of the very best NFL quarterbacks in the 1970s. He was the Peyton Manning or Tom Brady of his day. So while playing football for the United States Naval Academy, Staubach won the Heisman Trophy, which is given every year to the country's best college football player. It's also important to understand that anyone who graduates from a US military academy (Army, Air Force, Navy) receives free tuition in return for a service commitment of five years of active duty. After graduating in 1965, Staubach could have served his time in the US but signed up for a one-year tour of duty in Vietnam where he was a supply corps officer. He returned to the US in 1967 and finished out his military commitment, finally joining the Cowboys in 1969 as a 27-year-old rookie and played for 11 years.

So what did Roger Staubach do during the off-season? Count his money? Lay around on a beach? Make personal appearances? Shine his Super Bowl Rings? No. In an interview with the *Wall Street Journal*, Staubach says he started working in real estate in the off-season while he was a rookie player.

He didn't know how long his sports career would last, so he took a job at a real estate company to make sure he could support his children in case he got hurt or football didn't work out.

He had sought out one of the most successful real estate investors in Texas, Henry S. Miller, and asked for a meeting. He told the gentleman that he was interested in getting into real estate management and development and offered to work for free (volunteer) in exchange for mentorship. Miller agreed. Staubach put in the time to learn the craft of real estate management preparing himself for later life. After his career was over he transitioned seamlessly into the field and became an incredible success, selling his real estate firm in 2008 for $640 million.

For those who thought: *I can't afford to work for free and clearly he could*, sorry for the lack of sympathy, but that is simply nothing more than an excuse. There's a way to do everything—there's a way around every obstacle. You can always arrange your life to make time for what's most important to you, even when you're not getting paid. It's simply a matter of desire and willingness to view the situation in a positive light. If you focus on the fact that you won't get paid when you volunteer, you are focusing on the wrong thing. Focus on the benefits, not the burdens.

Focus on the benefits, not the burdens.

A young woman named Tina[1] was hired at the website Yelp. She wanted to work in media and took the job with great enthusiasm.

[1] Not her real name.

Unfortunately, the starting salary at Yelp was a problem for Tina. She lived alone and found it difficult to survive comfortably on what she earned. So in an unprecedented move, Tina wrote an open letter to the CEO of Yelp and posted it online. In the letter she complained about the poor starting pay and the difficulties it was causing her. She stated that after paying her rent she had very little left over for food and/or entertainment. She implored the CEO of Yelp to increase the pay for those starting out at the company as it would make their lives easier and, in essence, make them better employees.

Within two hours of posting her letter online she was fired. You may find this heartless, but I completely agree with Yelp's response. Tina didn't choose to find a way to go around the obstacles she encountered, she just complained about them. Tina certainly could have gotten a roommate, secured a second job, moved into a less expensive apartment, etc. If her dreams and desires were strong enough, Tina would have found a way to make this job work. Instead, she was confronted with an obstacle and did nothing to overcome it except to complain.

Now let's look at someone who encountered an obstacle on his journey to success and decided to do what needed to be done.

Case in Point

Daymond John grew up in the city as the son of a single mother. As a young man he wanted to get into the apparel business, so he asked his mother if she would teach him how to sew. Of course his mother was happy to and once he learned some minimal skills, he recreated a tie-top hat he had seen in a rap video. His friends liked the hat, so John spent forty dollars on material to make several dozen. He sold them all in one day on a street corner in Queens, New York and made $800 in cash.

He knew he was onto something. So he asked his mother to show him how to sew other garments. Every spare moment was spent sewing and coming up with new designs that he thought people would like. But he had to make money while chasing his dream. Unlike Tina, he did what needed to be done. So while the world was being introduced to FUBU (For Us, By Us), John was working nights at Red Lobster as a waiter.

"No one had any idea that the owner of FUBU was selling them shrimp and grits at night," he said. John found a way because his desire was strong enough. Now he sits on top of an empire that was created with a dream, desire, and one sewing machine.

Earlier in the book I left you hanging about Sara Blakely, the creator of Spanx, and what she did to pursue her dream. Much like Daymond John she had a strong desire to succeed and was willing to do whatever necessary to make it happen. Even though she knew that her destiny was calling, Sara was smart enough to know that it couldn't take place overnight and that there was still work to be done. She also had to eat and stay alive while she was pursuing her destiny. So she kept her job selling fax machines by day and spent every spare hour she had at night and on the weekends developing her product. She taught herself about patents, visited clothing manufacturers, and experimented with materials and alternative designs. She often passed up social invitations and dates preferring to stay home and pursue her dream. In other words, just like Daymond John, and countless other self-made millionaires and billionaires, she put the time in.

As Will Smith says: "Whatever your dream is, every extra minute needs to be donated to that."

So volunteering comes in many forms. You can certainly make the argument that Daymond John was "volunteering" his time to learn how to sew because at that point he was not being paid. Same goes for Sara Blakely. So another way of thinking about volunteering is as an investment. And it very well may be the best investment you will ever make.

If you're really interested in some aspect of a business, consider volunteering so you can learn more about it. The reason volunteering is such an effective method of gaining the best experience is because virtually anyone will hire you for two reasons: one, it doesn't cost them anything so there's no downside; and two, they respect and admire your willingness to learn and consequently are willing to teach you. You're investing your time in a way that will lead to later dividends. Once you get in the door it's a résumé builder, a great way to increase your knowledge base about a particular field, a limitless networking opportunity, and an entrée to the best possible, real-life working experience you could obtain.

Don't forget that the goal of this book is to provide you with stories and direction that you can learn from and then apply to further your goals. So, let me give you a few more examples of volunteering.

When Pat Croce first opened his SPORTS Physical Therapists rehabilitation center, he was looking for a unique way to advertise his services. His emphasis was not simply on treating injuries at his center, but on marketing sports training services to fitness-minded Americans. So he put his desire in the forefront of his mind and came up with an ingenious slant on the concept of volunteering. He offered to train Pierre Robert, a popular Philly deejay, for free.

So Croce put in the time and really worked hard at helping Robert get into shape, the same as he did with his paying clients. Lo and behold, the radio host loved how he felt and looked and went on the air to tell everyone what a great personal trainer Croce was and how terrific his center was. He couldn't have paid for better or more effective advertising. Pat Croce bet on himself and won.

My turn again. Here's an example of taking these lessons I learned from Pat Croce and applying them to my own life. Please look to this vignette as a road map when you decide you want to get your foot in the door of any profession.

Business at my law firm was thriving, and I was doing well financially, but something was missing in my life. I didn't have any children at the time and felt like I needed something to fill that void. I had always loved sports and played football in college, so I decided to get into coaching. (It all starts with a decision.) More specifically, I wanted to coach college football, and I wanted to be a quarterbacks' coach, inasmuch as I had played the position and felt that I could offer something of value to young players (confident clarity).

At that moment, because of everything I've already explained to you, I believed absolutely that I would be able to achieve this goal. (Eliminate any limiting beliefs.) But you have to buy a ticket (take action). Since I decided that I would have a better chance if it was a small college, I went online and searched local colleges with football teams. I found a small school that I had never even heard of, and it was only several miles from my office. I emailed the head coach that very night. I was polite, explained who I was, gave him some background information, and stated that I very much wanted to get into coaching. (Please make note that I had absolutely no coaching experience at all. Zero.)

Remembering Roger Staubach and Pat Croce, I wrote: "And to be clear, I'm not looking for any money at all. I'm more than willing to do this as a volunteer, and you have my word that I will never act like anything other than a full time, dedicated member of the staff."

I decided to make an investment and bet on myself.

Just as I outlined in a previous chapter, I requested a meeting at his convenience and thanked him in advance for his time. I received a return email the very next day, a Monday, with an invitation to meet with him on Tuesday. I went, we had lunch, and I walked out as the new quarterbacks' coach.

In less than 48 hours, I went from making the decision to be a college coach to securing a position as a college coach, without having any experience at all in the field of coaching. And if that head coach had not responded to my email or had he written back that he wasn't interested, I would have called him to change his mind, or I would have tried another school. Either way, I was going to get the position I wanted because I believed I would, and I took action to make it happen. It's an unbeatable combination, and it works every time.

Another way to view volunteering is as an on-the-job audition.

Please remember that I don't ever write about my own experiences to impress you but to impress upon you how these concepts work every single time.

Another way to view volunteering is as an on-the-job audition. If the decision makers are impressed with you and your work ethic and they see that you fit in, they are going to be more inclined to hire you than someone they don't know. Even if they have no room for you, they will be a great resource for a letter of recommendation or to suggest you to a friend or colleague as someone they should look to hire. Add the experience you're getting and it's a win-win.

But there is a catch. For it to be a winning relationship, you have to bring value to the job. This is a critical point. You are not entitled to slack off, be lazy, or be undependable because you are not getting paid. That type of attitude defeats the whole concept behind volunteering as an investment in your future.

To maximize the return on your investment you should not only bring value to the job, but be aggressive about asking to be part of as much as possible. Be the opposite of lazy. Do it respectfully and with due deference, but ask if you can attend that meeting . . . go on the site inspection . . . read the proposal . . . be at the real estate closing. It shows initiative and a desire to learn, two things that employers absolutely covet in employees. And it will be even more impressive as the decision makers constantly remind each other: *And they're doing all this without being paid.* All of a sudden you become the measuring stick by which other employees are evaluated. Soon enough you are the star employee who is getting paid—and paid well.

You might also think at this point: *I thought the whole idea was not to merely work for a company and make what they're willing to pay me?* Don't get confused. Working for a company is great as long as you're gaining experience and connections that you will use to reach great heights in your career or to create a business of your own.

Before ending this chapter, I want to take a moment to deal with one issue that can be a blind spot for young adults. When resources are limited, younger people tend to look at the cost of a book, or a seminar, or an online class as a deterrent. You have to fight through this. Keep your eye on the prize. What is more important, the ten dollars in your pocket or the how-to knowledge in that book that will help you attain your goals? Always view such a purchase as an investment.

I first learned this lesson when I was in my last year of law school and the time came to start submitting my résumé to firms looking to hire new attorneys. Back then a starting salary for a new lawyer was around $70,000, which was about four times as much as I was making as a clerk. I had done well academically in law school, winning an award for oral advocacy, making the law review (in essence a writing competition), and was about to graduate cum laude. So there I was thinking that the résumé I created sounded pretty good.

So I sent it out to a few dozen firms, then lo and behold . . . nothing. I didn't get a single interview. Classmates without all the achievements I had on my résumé were getting interviews, but I was not. I couldn't understand it for the life of me. How could this be? It didn't make sense. Then I saw an advertisement for a company that specialized in creating a more professional looking résumé, but the fee was one hundred dollars.

Now this was at a time when I didn't have any spare money. As I described at the beginning of the book, I was just barely skating by, picking what bills I would pay and which I would hold onto for a while. So I speak from experience when I say I get it. It's hard to spend money like that. But I really thought about it. I wasn't getting anywhere with the résumé that I created, and since my law school career was over, I didn't see anything that I could academically do to improve my stats. I really didn't know how to write a résumé, or what it should look like, or how to distinguish it from anyone else's. So I made the decision to find the money, which took a little doing, and invest it in this service.

I remember my meeting with the gentleman and how he looked at the content of my résumé. He was very complimentary but didn't like the layout.

He said confidently, "We can make this look better."

A week later I had his version, which looked terrific. The fonts, the use of bullet points, and the border he placed around the content really looked slick. And it is a fact that every single firm that received that résumé offered me an interview. Every one. I still had the same stats, but the look of that résumé seemed to make all the difference.

You need to learn this lesson right now. Don't be cheap at the expense of your future. Just ask yourself if what you're buying is an investment in your future. If the answer is yes, by all means invest the money.

Don't be cheap at the expense of your future.

I would like to add one little tip that I think makes a difference. Start your career the right way; pay for the book or the seminar. Don't conspire with a group so that one person pays for it, and then everyone just copies it. Integrity matters in all things, but it is an especially important factor when starting a venture. Never start anything in deceit. It's bad karma. And that goes for personal relationships, business ventures—whatever. If you begin in deceit I personally believe you are destined for failure.

I believe in this approach sincerely. Whenever a telemarketer calls my law firm and lies about their identity so I'll get on the phone with them, I end the conversation immediately and tell them straight out that I will never start a business venture with anyone who uses deceit at the beginning. No matter what. Don't do the right thing some of the time; do the right thing all of the time.

The Takeaway

- ✔ Volunteering is an investment in your future.
- ✔ How much you're being paid should never determine how hard you work.
- ✔ Never start any venture in deceit.
- ✔ Don't do the right thing some of the time; do the right thing all of the time.

TASK: Identify a way to volunteer your time so you can gain real-world, practical experience that will help you attain your ultimate goal. Saying you don't have the time is a cop out. How badly do you want it?

6

Attitude Is Everything

Nothing great was ever achieved without enthusiasm.

—Ralph Waldo Emerson

Attitude is an essential element of success. Malcom Forbes, founder of *Forbes* magazine, once explained that if he had an employee who was a top producer, a money maker, and a real winner but had a bad attitude, he'd fire him immediately. That is a great example of just how important your attitude is in the pursuit of success.

Ralph Waldo Emerson, addressing the graduating class of Harvard in the 1880s said famously: *Nothing great was ever achieved without enthusiasm*. The more passion and enthusiasm you can bring to your job, the more valuable you are, and the more successful you will become.

You see, attitude is always infectious. If someone has a great attitude, it lifts the spirits of everyone around them and as a result, benefits the whole. If someone has a bad attitude, it creates a vortex of negativity and depression that sucks in all around it and weakens the whole.

Attitude is always infectious.

There is an atmosphere in every workplace, whether it's a

bank, a law firm, a construction site, or an international think tank. No matter what type of atmosphere may exist, you have to take ownership of the energy that you bring into any space you enter. If you're negative, pessimistic, tired, disgusted, or a naysayer by nature, you will not thrive, and in general people won't enjoy your company. That type of attitude never inspires confidence in others and acts as an emergency brake hindering the group as well as your own forward motion.

It's also a symptom of a larger problem. I personally don't know many people who are successful yet hate what they do. One of the steps towards being successful is to have enthusiasm for your job. You've heard the saying: *Those who love what they do never work a day in their life.* Well, it's absolutely true. And it really makes perfect sense when you break it down. If you love what you do, you'll have a positive attitude toward it. Colleagues and underlings alike will find you pleasant to be around and feed off that positivity, becoming that much more energized and productive. Everyone works harder and longer because it doesn't seem like work when you're emotionally invested in something you love. Do what you love and the money will follow.

Those who love what they do never work a day in their life.

There's a line from the film *The Flamingo Kid*, where a father tells a son: *There are only two things that are important in life: finding out what you love, and finding out what you're good at. And if God is smiling on you, they're both the same thing.*

I would say it a little differently. I would put it this way: find what you love, and then enjoy learning to become great at it. In other words, it's up to you to take what you're passionate about and turn that passion into profit. It's far easier and more commonplace than you think because once you love something it's all made easier. You will go from loving it to becoming truly great at it, regardless of what the *it* is. Profits will follow passion and a positive attitude as surely as night follows day.

At this point in the book, I hope that you're starting to put all the pieces together. A can-do attitude is a positive attitude and essential to the attainment of success. So if your words and actions are positive, you will immediately start to attract positive things as well as inspire those around you. But if you allow yourself to be negative in your words, thoughts, or actions, you'll doom yourself to a life of struggle. And if you worked for Malcolm Forbes, you'd be fired already.

You have to take action; fortunately, if you're doing something that inspires you, taking action is the easy part. The more difficult challenge is to recognize and manage fear, often an impostor cloaked as endless excuses, which will only act to hold you back. But let's get back to attitude.

Earlier we discussed Roger Staubach. Imagine a quarterback getting into the huddle with two minutes left in the game with his team losing by four points. He looks at the guys and says: *Let's be honest, we really haven't played well all game, and I can't imagine that we're going to be able to magically turn that around now. We'll do our best but, we're probably going to lose. But we have the ball so we might as well try anyway. Let's run 800 Z post.*

How much confidence would that inspire in you? Do you think that his team would have a good chance to win in dramatic fashion? They would be doomed before they even snapped the ball for the play.

But what if the quarterback ran into the huddle, looked at the guys with a glint in his eye, and said: *We've got this. Let's make this stadium rock. In about a minute and a half, we're going to be in the end zone down there showing them how to celebrate a score. All you have to do is believe. We're in it together, and there is no place I'd rather be. Now let's go make history. Let's run 800 Z post.*

How about now? Do they have a chance to win? The answer is no; they don't have a chance to win . . . they are going to win.

In these scenarios we have the exact same players in the exact same situation. But the quarterback in the second hypothetical is positive, enthusiastic, and inspiring others to follow his lead. Conversely, I wouldn't follow the first quarterback no matter where he was going. I'll take my chances with the person who has the positive attitude every single time.

Emotions are a curious thing. Most people believe that you are who you are and consequently these same people think that you can't control your emotional response to a situation. But that isn't true. It's challenging to master your emotions for sure, but absolutely doable. You are in complete control over how you react to any situation. You can't stop the bad news from coming, but how you react to it is entirely up to you.

Arnold Schwarzenegger once gave an interview and said if he looked outside and noticed that his car had been stolen, he wouldn't care at all. He might call the insurance company, but that would be it. Getting mad or upset wouldn't get his car back and would in fact be a waste of time.

Okay, now if your first thought is that Arnold Schwarzenegger is rich and that's why he doesn't care, you're missing the point. He has mastered his emotions and understands that getting mad changes nothing. It is truly, as he described, a waste of time.

Related to this same concept of controlling your emotions, one seemingly impenetrable roadblock to success is when a person convinces themselves that they can't move forward because of some previous event that caused pain in their life.

It could be a troubled upbringing, a failed relationship, an accident, injury, or handicap that has altered their life, leaving them emotionally scarred.

Living in the past is one of the very worst things you can do. Please don't ever become a prisoner to the past no matter what misfortune befell you. I realize this may sound cold, but please give the logic behind it due consideration.

Your father left when you were a child? Endeavor never to do that to your child, and then move on.

You have a handicap? Don't accept it as an excuse. Work with what you have to do something great.

Your girlfriend broke your heart? There is a better match out there for you. Move on as soon as you can.

You were bullied as a child and the memories of it still adversely affect you? Well, then stop thinking about it. Catch these thoughts when they start, and actively replace them with something positive.

Dwelling on any negative aspect of your past is a straight waste of time. Don't ever let someone or something live in your head rent free. Evict them immediately, and get on with living your life. There's a reason why the windshield in your car is so big and the rearview mirror is so small: looking forward is that much more important than looking backward. And if you need professional help to move on from some misfortune, take action and seek out that help at once so you can start living a fruitful, passionate life sooner rather than later. After you examine a negative event from every angle and are able to fully deal with the pain it caused you, do you know what

There's a reason why the windshield in your car is so big and the rearview mirror is so small: looking forward is that much more important than looking backward.

the therapist will tell you? Move on. And this goes for things that happened two years ago or two hours ago.

One night I came home in a very bad mood. Someone had done something that really upset me. I started telling my wife, and I was like a truck going downhill. I got even more upset as I retold the whole story. My wife politely listened but gave me a look like I was being silly, which just made me frustrated with her, asking if she fully understood what I had just told her.

She said, "I understand the issue, but I guess I just don't understand why you would ever let a bad day ruin your night."

That sentence significantly changed my life. It seemed like a throwaway line, but the more I thought about it the more embarrassed I became. I thought: *Am I that weak that I would choose to stew in anger over something that already happened, that I can't change, and allow it to adversely affect not only my night, but my family's night, too? I'm going to foist my inability to control my emotions on my wife and son and make them have a bad night too?*

I realized that was just plain stupid. I took a moment to regroup and said, "You're right. Come on, I'll take you out for dinner." And we had a nice time.

Attitude is everything in the workplace, with your family, and when it comes to your own mental health. You are in charge of your emotions and can choose to have any attitude you like. You can live in the past and be miserable, ripping open the same scab time and again, or you can choose to move on and focus on the future you want to have.

You are in charge of your emotions and can choose to have any attitude you like.

You can view volunteering as strictly doing something for free, or you can see it as the investment it is.

You can focus on the beauty of the

destination or keep talking about how lengthy and uncomfortable the flight will be.

You can stay upset because of your bad day, or you can choose to enjoy your night. The choice is yours.

You can even make a mundane job seem exciting depending on your attitude and point of view.

So, let me leave this chapter with a parable of sorts to illustrate my point. A young man gets a job at a quarry. He shows up the first day and is met by a supervisor who offers to take him on a tour. The first person they come upon is a middle-aged man and he's breaking rocks with a sledge hammer. The new employee says hello and asks the man how he's doing.

The man responds in a surly tone: "How does it look like I'm doing? I'm too old to be breaking rocks for a living. And it's hotter than hell out here."

The new employee is a little startled by the man's dejection and thinks: *Do I want this to be my future?*

He continues on and sees another man who is supposed to be doing the same job. This man is checking his watch and only starts barely hitting the rocks as the supervisor comes into view. The young employee doesn't even bother to ask how he's doing because the man is wearing it all over his face: he's miserable too. The supervisor then brings the new employee over to meet the man he'd be replacing.

"We're promoting this man you're about to meet. He's going to be in charge of one of our other quarries," the supervisor said.

They turned the corner and the new employee saw a man hitting rocks with a sledge hammer like his life depended on it. The rocks splintered apart because of the sheer force of his blows. And he wore a grin.

"How are you doing, young man? I hear that you're going to be my replacement."

The new employee nodded, a little taken aback by the man's enthusiasm. "Yes, I'm here to break rocks."

The worker struck another rock. "Oh, that's too bad. I'm sorry to hear that."

The new employee looked puzzled. "I thought that was the job: breaking rocks. Isn't that what you're doing?"

The man stopped hitting his rock and looked at his would-be replacement for a moment. "Not at all. I mean, there are a few guys here who break rocks, but me? I'm building a cathedral."

The Takeaway

- ✔ Attitude is everything. A positive attitude will bring happiness and success while a negative one guarantees you misery and failure.
- ✔ Be enthusiastic in pursuing your dream.
- ✔ You are in control of how you react to each and every situation. Rule your emotions; don't let your emotions rule you.

TASK: Go through an entire day without uttering a single negative comment about anything. Stay completely positive for one whole day.

7

Remove Yourself from Negativity

Impossible is an opinion.

—Mohammad Ali

There are two types of people who will always tell you that you can't do something: those who are too afraid to try themselves and those too afraid that you'll succeed. Given this unfortunate reality, I have no choice but to dedicate one small section of this book to something we can't control: other people's negativity. All negativity is a vortex. It sucks people into a funnel of doom and despair. You have to limit how much negativity you're exposed to because like a cancer left unchecked, it will grow and ultimately take hold of you.

It is my sincere hope that you see real value in this book and become an absolute devotee of this philosophy to never allow yourself to say or think a negative thought. But that doesn't mean that those around you will act in kind, including family. You love your brother, mother, sister, or whomever, but they're naysayers, depressive personalities, or just plain negative. How you limit the time you spend with people you love and/or live with is a vexing question.

The answer is you really can't. But my suggestion is to limit what you discuss with them. If you are excited about an idea or a venture and you know that someone will mock it, question your abilities to succeed, or ridicule you for it, why discuss it with them?

To be clear: I never want anyone to be anything but honest with me when discussing one of my ideas or projects. I often preface my request for their opinion by saying: *Please don't tell me what I want to hear; I'd rather you be brutally honest.* There is a difference between constructive criticism based on knowledge and/or experience and knee-jerk negativity from someone with a habit of naysaying. This brings us back to the earlier point that you should only ask advice of people who have something of value to offer in the area you're discussing.

Let's look at it from a different angle. If I discuss an idea with someone and that person says it'll never work, the next question becomes pivotal: why?

If the person says it just won't, I disregard it immediately and entirely. I don't mind thoughtful criticism and have learned a great deal from other people's critiques, but I have no time at all for baseless negativity. And you shouldn't either. If the person you are speaking with can't articulate why they have a negative opinion of your idea, plan, or goal, keep moving forward without paying a second's attention to what they said because in effect they said nothing.

You have to limit the amount of time you spend with negative people because it can only harm your attitude, outlook, and enthusiasm.

As we've discussed, most successful people are engaging, positive, energetic, and dynamic while unsuccessful people tend to be surly, negative, pessimistic, and one-dimensional. You have to limit the amount of time you spend with negative people because it can only harm your attitude, outlook, and enthusiasm.

And here is the kicker: negative people rarely ever recognize it in themselves. If you politely asked someone why they tend to view things so negatively, the likely response you'll get is: *What are you talking about? I'm not negative, I'm a realist,* which is nothing more than a rationalization. They don't see it, won't acknowledge it, and consequently, can't stop doing it.

I hate that guy . . . . Doesn't anyone working here know what they're doing? . . . Nothing works out for people like us . . . . It will probably rain on my day off . . . . How are you going to make money with that idea? . . . Can you believe I had to park two blocks away from my favorite restaurant?

They see the negative side of every situation. Instead of focusing on how delicious the meal will be or how nice it is to have friends and family to share a night out with, they obsess about how long the wait will be or how parking is sure to be a problem. You have to actively guard against letting this attitude negatively influence your thinking.

Someone who really understands the importance of being positive and the need to eliminate all things negative is Carolyn Rafaelian. You'll recall that she started the wildly successful jewelry company Alex and Ani that went from zero dollars in sales to $350 million in sales in less than a decade. Their website touts: *Positive energy as a core company belief.* Every bangle, bracelet, and ring is *infused with positive intention* to aid all those who wear it. She's tapped into the vital importance of remaining positive and is bringing it to the masses in the form of jewelry.

I'm hoping to do something similar with this book. You see, negative people are like dark, dank clouds that hang over you, while positive people are like brilliant sunshine. The more time you spend in the sunshine, the better off and happier you will be. And let me give you another warning: Negative people love to lump you in with them. It makes them feel better to think that you won't succeed either. In some cases, it may be subconscious, but they want to crush your dreams nonetheless because they don't have any of their own.

Remember, when you ask a negative person for advice, it's likely that they will try to foist their limiting beliefs on you. Don't let that happen. Be confident and move forward.

Case in Point

I once handled a case where a two-year-old boy walked out the front door of a daycare center without anyone noticing he was missing. Unfortunately, that case ended in tragedy when the boy found his way to the building's roof and fell to his death. It was a heartrending case to be part of and seemed so senseless. How could a child in a daycare center walk right out the front door without anyone knowing?

But after I started doing some research I learned that daycare centers aren't allowed to lock the doors, or even use child locks, in case there is a fire. So how do you guard against children walking out the front door if it's left open? The more research I did the more I found that children wandering out of daycare centers and private homes is a very common occurrence. It only takes a second for a caretaker to get distracted and tragedy to strike, like it did in this case.

After the case was over, I kept thinking about the situation and wondered out loud why there wasn't a device such as a small bracelet that a child could wear that would alert the caretaker if they move beyond a designated area. Something akin to a door alarm in a department store but much simpler.

I shared my idea with numerous people I respected, and every one of them said they must have that already.

But I did not let that deter me in the least. I did exhaustive research and found that there was no such item offered for sale. My idea was unique. Still, virtually every person tried to dissuade me from developing such a product.

You don't know anything about engineering. You're a lawyer, not an inventor. What do you know about radio frequency?

And on and on and on. Drawing on the principles from this book, I was completely undeterred. I hired an MIT engineer to do a study as to whether the product could work and what the projected cost was to create it. I hired a patent attorney to file the specs with the patent office in Washington, DC, and I hired a company to design the look of the product and develop promotional materials.

At this very moment that product is being shopped around to major companies. When it goes into production, I am going to take great satisfaction knowing that I turned an idea into a reality, that I ignored all the naysayers, and that I created a product that will save lives. And I will get paid handsomely for what I created.

As with all examples in this book, I do not tell you to impress you, but to impress upon you the importance of the concepts in this book. The truth is, I didn't know anything about radio frequency devices, engineering, product development, patents, etc. I made it my business to learn. I found out that most of it was simple, and I was able to hire people to do the things that were beyond my capabilities. From the inception of my idea to the development of promotional materials and prototypes, I spent less than $6,000.

Nothing is beyond your abilities if your desire is strong enough.

Nothing is beyond your abilities, if your desire is strong enough.

The Takeaway

✔ Do your very best to avoid any and all forms of negativity.

✔ If you can't avoid those who are negative, you have to make yourself impervious to their negativity.

✔ Water cannot sink a ship unless it gets inside; don't let it in.

TASK: Identify the members of your immediate family and five other people you spend the most time with. Then determine whether each person is a positive or negative influence on you.

8

Good Manners Are Essential

Good manners will open doors that the best education cannot.

—Supreme Court Justice Clarence Thomas

How you treat people is also critically important to your chances of success in life, and this is absolutely a lost art. I'm not exactly sure when rudeness became our baseline approach as a society, but that's where we currently are. When you think of the elements necessary to obtain a certain enviable level of success, people tend to think about education, inventiveness, diligence, genius, etc., as the pieces that need to fall into place. Rarely do you hear anyone refer to manners, courtesy, kindness, and compassion as being key components to reaching the top. But they are.

As a person who's made his living as a negotiator for the past 22 years, I can tell you that how you treat people is at the very core of whether or not you will be successful. I find it absolutely astonishing so few people realize this very basic fact. Whether you are dealing with your spouse, an airline flight attendant, the mechanic fixing your car, a cashier, an insurance adjuster, or someone painting your house, your treatment of that person will determine the outcome of the encounter every time. I truly believe that if you're nice to a thief, they will be less likely to rob you. I'm not kidding; that's how strongly I believe in the importance of treating people with respect.

I was at an airport recently and found out that my flight would be delayed. I went up to the ticket counter, stood in line, and listened as passenger after passenger berated this young lady.

I have to be in Boston by 6:00. . . . I have a wedding to go to. . . . Why can't they get another plane? . . . I want to speak to a manager. . . . You're useless. . . . I'll never use this airline again.

On and on. Now it was my turn. I stepped up to the counter. "You have a really hard job." I could see the young woman's body relax.

"You mean you're not going to yell at me?"

I said, "Let me ask you a question: is it your fault that the plane is late?"

She shook her head as fast as she could. "Not at all."

I smiled. "Then why on earth would I yell at you? I was just hoping for a status update in case I need to make arrangements."

She returned my smile, reached under the counter, and handed me hundreds of dollars of coupons to be used toward future flights. "This is for being so nice."

That's an example of how low we've sunk as a society. I received a substantial benefit for merely being nice.

Why do we think that yelling at someone, insulting them, threatening them, or being rude to them is the best way to get what we want? It's foolish. Truth is, people tend to dig in when confronted and soften when they discern that you don't want to argue with them. Want something done in a hurry? Tell the person: *I know you're busy, so please feel free to get to it when you can.* Want good service at a restaurant? Ask the waiter or waitress their name, and then introduce everyone at your table. These tiny, common courtesies are so appreciated, and you'll be shocked at the response you receive.

If you distill it down, when you're nice to someone you're showing appreciation and everyone wants to be appreciated. But it's even more than that. This funny thing happens when you show kindness to most people: they respond in kind. All of a sudden, they can't do enough for you.

I think there would be fewer divorces if husbands occasionally said: *You know, you do so much around here, and I want you to know how much I appreciate it. It's a big job, and you really do it well, and that's on top of working at a full-time job. I notice, and I really do appreciate it. Thank you.*

Or if women occasionally said to their husbands: *We are very lucky as a family to have you. We never miss a meal, are warm in the winter, and have everything we need because of how hard you work. I know it's not easy, but it is appreciated. Thank you.*

When you hear words like that, you don't mind working hard so that everyone else can have what they need. It's the difference between feeling mere obligation as opposed to joy in providing for loved ones.

Now let's switch it around. *I don't give a damn that you work too. Cleaning the house is your responsibility, and the place is a pigsty. Have some pride and clean up around here.*

I don't know of many wives who would warmly embrace their husband after that was said.

All you do is work, work, work, but I don't see it paying off. We're struggling like hell because you can't seem to advance at your job. You either need to work harder or find something you're better at.

Should this woman expect flowers the next day? How you treat people will always bear on the outcome.

Does a friendly demeanor help in business? The answer is a resounding yes. First of all, just like a positive attitude, friendliness and good manners make you instantly more likable.

People universally love to be treated with respect and kindness and will almost always respond in kind.

People universally love to be treated with respect and kindness and will almost always respond in kind. But don't be confused. Integrity and competence can go hand-in-hand with friendliness and good manners. If you remember nothing else from this chapter, remember this: if you are unlikable, you present a significant barrier to getting what you want. If people don't care for you, they will fight you and will often go out of their way to cause you problems. If, on the other hand, you are likeable, they will go out of their way to help you. It's really that simple.

Did you ever have someone pull their car up, roll down the window, and yell: *Where's Main Street?* Why on earth would I want to help that guy? He's asking for a favor but can't ask any nicer than that?

Excuse me . . . Sorry to bother you . . . Pardon me . . . Would you happen to know how to get to Main Street?

Any of these are acceptable and make me want to help. The nicer you ask, the better chance you have of obtaining what you want, whether it's something as simple as directions or something far more valuable. Let me give you a real-world example of how honesty, integrity, and simply being nice can equal a financial windfall.

Case in Point

I went to law school with a guy who I ultimately became friends with. We stayed friends for many years, even though we didn't see each other often. He came upon a great real estate opportunity and offered to let me in on it. I didn't have any experience with real estate development, but we were friends and liked each other so I accepted his offer and we purchased a piece of commercial real estate together.

Ultimately, after trying unsuccessfully to sell the property, we agreed to lease it to a third party. The very next day, like a gift from God, a big European company offered to buy the property for a lot of money. But we had already leased it to someone else and that prevented us from saying yes to the sale. I told my partners that I would go and speak to the leaseholder to see if he would let us back out of the deal.

How are you going to do that? they asked.

I merely responded, "Leave it to me."

The truth was that I knew exactly what approach I was going to use—complete honesty—and didn't want to risk hearing any negative feedback.

I set up a meeting with this very successful, hard-boiled businessman and said, "Something has happened that we weren't anticipating. At the very outset I want you to know that we have a deal, and we will absolutely abide by it if that's what you ultimately want. That said, a large company just offered us a lot of money for the property, so financially speaking, we would do much better to sell it as opposed to lease it. Is there any way that you would consider letting us do that?"

"But where else can I move my business?" he asked.

I didn't hear no.

I said, "I realize that if you pass on the lease it

would help us but hurt you. What if we were to give you some money out of the proceeds of the sale to help you with the inconvenience and thank you for letting us have the deal?"

He said, "You tell your partners that when a young man looks me in the eye and tells me the truth, all I want to do is help him. Go ahead and make your deal. I don't want to stand in your way."

———————————————————————

That story is 100 percent true. But you need to understand why I chose to approach the gentleman as I did. First off, I wanted him to know that this was a new development that could not have been anticipated. Secondly, and this was the pivotal part of the approach, I wanted to establish that I was honorable and would abide by the agreement if he needed it. I didn't say: *We feel the lease has loopholes*, or *We'll litigate if need be*, or any other type of veiled threat to try and scare him or make it adversarial.

Quite to the contrary. I told him in essence that we would not try to wiggle out of our agreement for any reason. I then offered complete honesty and told him exactly why selling the property was preferential to us—because we would make more money. When he responded by saying: *Where else can I move my business?* I drew on what I had learned from Pat Croce and didn't hear no.

The last part is also important. I realized that I had to offer him something for any inconvenience, and as a token of appreciation, if he decided to let us out of the lease. We did, in fact, give him a considerable sum of money out of our sale as an acknowledgment of what he had done for us. So in other words, there were obstacles, but I found a way around them.

There's a way to solve every problem.

People respond as well to honesty and character as they do good manners and friendliness. I venture to guess that most people in that situation would have gone for the more aggressive *We'll tie you up in court for years* route, and I'm sure that's what he expected. But that approach was far less likely to work and was at its core dishonorable, which is no way to conduct yourself in business.

> **There's a way to solve every problem.**

Remember this: impress someone with character and they'll tell 10 people about it; upset someone by being dishonorable and they'll tell one thousand people about it. Reputation is extremely important because that is what will precede you into the next deal. You don't want anyone ever saying: *I heard you were dishonest and not to be trusted* or *Oh my God, you're John Smith? I heard you were a real jerk to deal with.* In either respect you will have created barriers that will be hard to overcome.

The Takeaway

✔ Manners matter and character is everything.

✔ There's a solution to every problem.

TASK: Go through an entire day smiling at everyone you see, and be polite to everyone you meet. I guarantee you'll be pleasantly surprised at how nice everyone will be in return.

Perseverance Always Wins

I am not the richest, smartest, or most talented person in the world, but I succeed because I keep going and going and going.

—Sylvester Stallone

Perseverance can be your greatest asset. It is greater than talent, privilege, or even education.

Perseverance can be your greatest asset. It is greater than talent, privilege, or even education. This simple statement can change your life.

Steve Jobs, the founder of Apple, famously said: *I'm convinced that about half of what separates the successful entrepreneurs from the unsuccessful ones is perseverance.*

And if you really think about it, shouldn't it be that way? If a person has a great idea for a new product and then abandons all efforts to develop it after only a few weeks or a few negative comments about it from some friends, does that person deserve to be wildly successful? Did they really even earn any right to be disappointed in their failed venture?

Everyone knows that Thomas Edison changed the world forever when he invented the lightbulb. What most people don't know is that he had more than 10,000 failed attempts before he successfully created an item that is used in every home, business, and building all over the globe. Would you say that he earned his success?

Jack Canfield is the author of *Chicken Soup for the Soul* and a host of other wildly successful books. The initial manuscript of *Chicken Soup for the Soul* was rejected by 44 publishers. He probably had to borrow Stephen King's spike. Would you have stopped after the 25th version of the *Your book isn't good enough to be published by us* letter that you received? Would you have quit after the 30th rejection? If you did, you would have thrown away a great future as well as a franchise that's now estimated to be worth more than $100 million.

Prior to writing *Chicken Soup for the Soul,* Canfield was a teacher. I add that not because there is anything wrong with being a teacher, but because he proves that a person is capable of changing their life and attaining astonishing wealth regardless of how modest their present circumstance may be—and that's without hitting the lottery.

But it takes perseverance, which comes in many different forms and can be placed under the *take action* heading. I once heard Canfield speak and he told this story: A young woman dreamed of attending graduate school at a particular institution. She worked hard, graduated college with great grades, and then applied to her dream school. Much to her surprise, she was rejected. Instead of being angry (a total waste of time), or depressed (understandable but equally wasteful), she wrote to the school and stated that she intended to reapply as many times as it would take to gain acceptance. She then asked what she could do during the intervening year that might aid her candidacy for the next time she applied.

Members of the selection committee convened to discuss her

letter and agreed to make room for her in their program without the need for her to reapply because they were so impressed with the resolve, desire to succeed, and perseverance she demonstrated.

One person I really admire is the late Jerry Weintraub, a film producer whose movies include *Oceans 11* and its two sequels. He is the absolute embodiment of virtually everything this book is about. Fellow acclaimed film director, Steven Soderbergh, did a biopic about him entitled *His Way*, which I strongly urge you to watch.

The first thing that jumped out at me was that some of the extremely successful people being interviewed, Brad Pitt for one, said that the secret to Jerry Weintraub's success is that he simply didn't hear the word no. In Jerry's world, no meant maybe and maybe meant we're closer to yes. Reflect on the true anecdote below and try to identify how and when he used concepts you've already read about in this book to become successful.

In Jerry's world, no meant maybe and maybe meant we're closer to yes.

Case in Point

Jerry was a young man trying to break into show business as a manager. He was watching television one night and saw Elvis Presley perform. He then wrote down on a piece of paper: *Jerry Weintraub Presents Elvis.* He was so excited that he woke up his wife and told her that he was going to manage Elvis Presley. She looked at him like he was crazy.

You don't even know Elvis, how is it that you're going to be managing him? This is crazy. He's never going to let you be his manager.

The next day Jerry did a little research and found out that Colonel Tom Parker was Elvis's representative. Jerry got his number and called. Colonel Parker said he had never heard of Jerry Weintraub, Elvis was not in need of a promoter or manager, and promptly hung up on him.

Completely undaunted, Jerry called Colonel Parker every single morning for one year, being cordial in every instance even when the Colonel was not. But over time he started to break down the Colonel's negativity toward the venture and they even became, according to Jerry, phone buddies. In 1964, after a full year, the Colonel asked Jerry if he still wanted to take Elvis on the road and be his tour manager. Jerry, of course, accepted and then proved his worth by making it the most successful tour Elvis ever had. By the time the national tour ended, Jerry had earned $3 million.

So what did Jerry do that was previously explained in this book?

1. Confident clarity. (Jerry Weintraub Presents Elvis)
2. Our thoughts, particularly the ones we say out loud, forecast our destiny. (*Sweetheart, wake up. I'm going to be tour managing Elvis Presley.*)
3. Don't take or follow advice from people not qualified to give it. (*You don't know Elvis; this is crazy; he's never going to let you be his tour manager.*)
4. Take action no matter how small. (*I found out that I*

had to speak to a Colonel Tom Parker, and I got his phone number.)

5. He didn't say no. And if he did, Jerry didn't hear it. *(I've never heard of you; Elvis doesn't need and a manager; and you're not taking him on the road.)*

6. Perseverance. *(I called him every day for an entire year.)*

7. Be cordial in all dealings no matter what. (Jerry was cordial during every phone conversation even when the Colonel was not.)

8. Bring value to what you do. (Jerry orchestrated the most successful tour Elvis ever had.)

The above story is not only true, but just one of a thousand stories I could have written where the same principles came into play. The point is that perseverance is an important thing to remember when pursuing your passions and dreams, perhaps the most important. Few baseball players hit a home run the first time they step up to the plate. But how foolish would it be for any baseball player to go hitless in his first game and then quit because he failed?

Just like Steve Jobs said, perseverance is part of what often separates the successful entrepreneurs from the unsuccessful. Please remind yourself of Thomas Edison, Jack Canfield, Jerry Weintraub, and Stephen King if ever you meet some resistance, rejection, or even failure on your journey toward wealth and happiness. But all of the struggles listed above pale in comparison to the story of one famous American. Consider this résumé (the numbers in parenthesis represent his age at the time) and ask yourself if you would have been discouraged at any point:

+ failed in business (22)
+ ran for legislature; defeated (23)

- ✦ failed in business again (24)
- ✦ elected to the legislature (25)
- ✦ sweetheart died (26)
- ✦ had nervous breakdown (27)
- ✦ defeated for speaker of the house (29)
- ✦ defeated for elector (31)
- ✦ defeated for congress (34)
- ✦ elected to congress (37)
- ✦ defeated in reelection bid (39)
- ✦ defeated for the senate (46)
- ✦ defeated for vice president (47)
- ✦ defeated for senate (second time) (49)

But then in 1860, Abraham Lincoln was elected the 16th president of the United States.

The Takeaway

- ✔ Perseverance may be the single most important factor in attaining success.
- ✔ In business no means maybe, and maybe means you're a step away from yes.
- ✔ Even if you encounter failure just keep going. And going, and going.

TASK: Write down a time in your life you gave up on something. Read it several times, crumple up the paper, and throw it away with the belief that it will never happen again.

Believe It Will Happen

*It's all about believing. You don't need to
know how it will happen, just that it will.*

—Author unknown

There was something else amazing that Jerry Weintraub did. It is the single most difficult concept to explain and for people to understand and/or accept. The problem is one of terminology. I never liked hearing about energy, or the universe, or even the laws of attraction. And if you say it's God you immediately lose a certain percentage of people and anger a bunch more. But you have to call it something so let's just refer to it as *the concept*. But please focus on the fact that it works every time regardless of what it's called.

When the Colonel told Jerry that he could produce Elvis' tour after an entire year of phone calls, he attached two conditions to it: Jerry had to fly to Las Vegas the very next day and bring $1 million of good-faith money.

Jerry didn't have anywhere near that much money. He was a regular young guy trying to make his mark and had yet to hit it big. So how do you raise $1 million in a day when you're just a regular person? Or perhaps a better question is, could *you* raise

$1 million in 24 hours? If your answer was either no or *That would be impossible*, you have yet to sign onto the concept, so please read on.

The answer to most of your dreams lies within this chapter. Consider it next level thinking. I will grant you that it is difficult to believe in the concept, but it's so important to understand that it exists and is as available to you as it was to Jerry. I've used it countless times with tremendous success, and it doesn't cost a dime. My challenge is to give you the information in a way that you won't merely discount it as impossible, hard to believe, or downright ludicrous.

So here it is: whatever you truly believe will happen, will happen.

I alluded to it earlier with a story about Derek Jeter and discussed the importance of confident clarity, but what I'm talking about here is something beyond even faith; I'm talking about certainty. Acting, feeling, and believing

Whatever you truly believe will happen, will happen.

that something will happen even though you have absolutely no idea how it ever could. You not only have to believe that something will happen, but spend a little time every day feeling as though it already has. Use your imagination to see the end result. Just like Jerry Weintraub deciding that he would tour manage the then-biggest star in the world before he ever even met him, seeing the end result, and writing down what it would look like up on the marquee: *Jerry Weintraub Presents Elvis*.

Or Jim Carrey making out a $10 million check payable to himself and writing in a specific date in the future. All you have to do is understand the concept and employ some of the strategies detailed in this book. But you need not be famous to use the concept. Anyone can use it who understands it and follows the rules.

I've always counted myself lucky because I somehow innately understood that if I believed something would happen, it would. But how do you explain this concept to someone else without seeming crazy?

Do you really think you can spin the world in your direction? . . . Are you trying to tell us that you can just make things happen the way you want? . . . So all I need to do is believe it will happen and it will?

The answer to all of these is yes. And the answer remains yes even if you have no idea how you'll actually accomplish your goal. Now what follows are several true stories from my own life, and I'll admit that I don't find it easy writing about this. The natural reaction people have is to think you're blowing your own horn so others will think highly of you. But I can assure you that I have no interest in that. I'm choosing to write about my own experience here so you can see how I employed the concept as well as some of the other previously discussed tactics. Please read these anecdotes critically and try to figure out what you would have done in each instance, drawing on everything you've read up to now.

When my wife and I bought our home there was a fireplace in the living room with a blank wall over it. The way the room was situated made that area a real focal point, and I knew we needed to find something extraordinary. A few months later I was in a swanky area in Florida and stopped into an art gallery. There it was: the perfect painting. Every color, every brush stroke, the frame, the size—it was truly perfect. I could see every stick of furniture that would surround it. I could picture us sitting on our couch gazing at this beautiful piece of art. The decor would revolve around the color and style of this original oil painting. I absolutely had to have it; I mean, how often do you find perfect?

So I sought out the owner and inquired as to the price. The woman said, "Twenty thousand dollars, not just because it's beautiful, but because it's one of a kind."

I took a picture of it with my phone, said thank you, and left. I called my wife and said I had found our painting, it was perfect, and then sent her a picture of it.

She agreed. "How much?"

"Twenty thousand dollars."

Silence. "You're not actually considering that, are you?" she finally asked.

"I'm absolutely getting it, but I won't spend that much for it. I'll get it for $3,000."

Again, silence. "And just how are you going to do that?" she asked with a slight laugh.

"I just will," was all I said because I knew I just would.

Two weeks later I called the woman in Florida and told her I wanted to make a deal for the painting and then offered her $3,000. She laughed. I don't mean chuckled. She laughed at me.

"This is not Christmas nor your birthday, Mr. Colucci. The painting is $20,000."

I spoke to her politely and then hung up, but I was completely undaunted because I *knew* that I would ultimately get it. I didn't hear no. That painting was going to hang in my living room, that's all there was to it. I remained patient and willing to part with $3,000 to make that happen.

As my wife and I shopped for furniture we kept referring to our painting when it came to choosing the color and style of the other pieces in the room.

I don't think that sofa will look good with our painting . . . The colors will clash . . . and so forth.

This went on for seven months. During that time, my wife

would occasionally say things like: *Maybe we should just look for another painting* or *Do you see anything else working over the fireplace?*

But in each instance I would just shake my head no. *We've found the perfect painting. We'll have it.*

For nearly one year the focal point of the room remained blank, but all the furniture we did acquire was specifically chosen to go with, augment, and complement our painting. Around month 13 I emailed the seller and reiterated my offer of $3,000. I added that perhaps it was overpriced given that it still hadn't sold. She wrote me back a terse note, but did say that she would discount the painting if I truly wanted it. The compromised price would be . . . $19,000. I thanked her for her willingness to reduce her price, but stated that I would not pay more than $3,000.

Almost a year and half after I first saw the painting our wall was still blank. Sometimes I would sit in the living room with a smile, imagining how awesome our painting was going to look right over the fireplace accented by the art light that hung above it. After staring at our blank wall one night I went to bed but for whatever reason could not get to sleep, which is rare for me. So I played around on my iPad still thinking about our painting, and decided to look up the artist.

I searched his name and found out when he lived and died as well as some interesting facts about his work. I also saw a link to an auction that would include one of his original oil paintings. I clicked on that link, and there it was. Our painting. The original one of one would be auctioned off in New York City the following week. How it got to New York I have no idea.

The next morning, I nervously waited for my wife to wake up so I could turn the iPad around and show her what I had discovered. As soon as her eyes began to open, I was tapping the screen, directing her attention to my discovery.

"Is that our painting?" she blurted out, trying to focus on the screen despite not being fully awake.

"It is. And you and I are going to New York to get it."

So we went. We were able to verify that it was indeed the painting and would be auctioned off the following day. We were told we could bid by phone if we filled out all the paperwork, and with that we headed back to Boston.

Monday morning, just as anticipated, we received a call from the auction house saying that lot 201 was about to go on the block. The opening bid was $1,500. I offered $2,000. Another bidder offered $2,250, and I immediately responded with $2,400. We went up in hundred dollar increments until he said $2,900. I didn't even hesitate: $3,000.

I heard the young man relaying my bid over the phone say, "It is with you at $3,000 . . . Still with you at $3,000 . . . Auctioneer giving fair warning . . . Still with you at $3,000 . . . Sold to you for $3,000. Congratulations."

That painting hangs in my home in the place of honor, as it was always meant to, and will never be replaced. Not just because it's beautiful and an original work of art, but because it represents so much to me. It's the physical proof that the concept works every time. Desire, visualization, belief, a little action, and absolute persistence will yield what you want even if it seems impossible.

Desire, visualization, belief, a little action, and absolute persistence will yield what you want even if it seems impossible.

Now you might think that it was a fluke. So let me turn the tables and ask at what point would you have looked for another painting? And before you answer let me assure you that there will be a day when you'll happily part with $3,000 for something you really want. But the questions stands: at what point would have looked for another painting?

If you buy into the concept, the answer is never. When you fully grasp and employ the concept you'll realize that it's a foregone conclusion that you'll get whatever it is you want, and that it's just a matter of time and precious little else. Not a believer yet?

Case in Point

When Colonel Tom Parker told Jerry that he needed to bring $1 million to the International Hotel in Vegas in 24 hours, Jerry said no problem despite not having anywhere near that much money. But Jerry understood the concept better than most. He simply knew that he would get the money.

After several phone calls to people that he knew, none of whom were interested in such a deal, someone suggested that Jerry call a man in the northwest who owned radio stations and who also happened to be a big Elvis fan. Can you think of any set of circumstances less likely to produce success than Jerry calling someone he didn't know and asking him for $1 million so he could take Elvis, who he had never met nor spoken to, on tour? As unbelievable as that might sound to you, the radio station owner agreed after Jerry offered him half of everything he would ever make as a concert promoter. So the deal was struck.

I implore you to read, reread, and read again the entire Jerry Weintraub anecdote from start to finish. It truly exemplifies everything about the concept that I want you to buy into. And of all the things Jerry Weintraub did to make that particular dream a reality, calling the Colonel every day for a year is the most impressive. Persistence and belief have to be intertwined. The more you believe, the more persistent you will be, and success and riches will follow.

Remember, you don't need to be rich, famous, educated, connected, established, healthy, younger, older, or anything else to make use of this concept. You just need to forever change your mind-set to start attracting exactly the future and lifestyle that you want, one filled with wealth and fulfillment. The sooner you start making these changes the more of life there will be for you to enjoy. Just move forward with absolute belief that your goal will be attained without being consumed with how. And do it despite what your parents, teachers, or friends may think because it's not their dream; it's yours. I promise you, as surely as you are reading this book right now, the *how* will be revealed to you when you convince yourself that your goal will be attained.

Now, yet again, I provide stories from my own life to impress upon you how the concept works. I also hope that it's easier to accept that you too can use the concept by seeing that it can work for someone who is not a Hollywood star, movie producer, professional athlete, or famous author. I'm someone who grew up in modest circumstances and ultimately had so much student loan debt that I couldn't see any way that I would ever be able to afford a house. So I give you these vignettes to hopefully inspire you.

I was on vacation in Florida and walking down the street toward a coffee shop. I glanced at a realty office window as I passed by and noticed a picture, one of maybe 50, of a beautiful backyard. There was an exotic pool, an outdoor bar, and a lanai all surrounded by gorgeous, tropical landscaping. Then I looked at the other pictures of the home and thought that it was just like my painting—perfect. But then I looked at the price: $675,000. At the time I had amassed about $160,000, which may sound like a lot, but it took me 13 years working as a lawyer to earn that much money.

I went into the office and requested a showing. It was even better in real life. I loved it. *What an awesome second home*, I thought. I absolutely had to have that property.

I'm going to walk you through my thinking at the time.

Okay, I want this house, but I can't afford it. How do I do this?

First, I convinced myself that it would be mine. I started shopping for furniture online, took the floor plan and began organizing the furniture to make best possible use of the space. I put the real estate ad on my favorite places and looked at the pictures almost every day. I also put in my mind that I was going to pay cash for the home *and* not buy it until I had accumulated double the purchase price, so I would have enough money in reserve to be comfortable.

Please note that I had the desire first and convinced myself that the home would be mine before ever considering the how. Not only that, I made it twice as hard on myself by deciding that I wouldn't buy the home until I had double the purchase price.

After making the decision in my mind that I would someday own that house, I began to think about how I would attract that kind of money. I continuously thought that I would attract the money because I had to. I never worried about how, I just kept it in my mind.

One year later a friend of mine, completely out of the blue, offered to let me in on a real estate deal. He needed additional capital for a project and told me that I would get one third of his deal for an investment of $150,000. I did my due diligence, asked around, visited the site, looked at other sales in the area, and decided it was a great investment opportunity.

Let's stop here and take inventory.

I had worked for more than a decade to save $160,000, and I was looking at the prospect of risking virtually all of it on this investment. Was I scared? Initially, yes. But I realized that fear was nothing more than false events appearing real, so I took a step back, thought about everything I had researched and learned, and decided to act. I knew that this was the how, so I took the plunge.

We held the property for about one year before we had a contract to sell it for a handsome profit. By this time, two years had passed since I first saw the house I wanted to buy. During that entire time, I kept looking at my house in Florida and watched as the price slowly but steadily decreased. It went from $675,000 to $650,000 to $599,000 to $550,000 to $525,000. When all was said and done with my land deal, I would net out about $350,000 plus return of my initial investment of $150,000. So I was only $25,000 short of the purchase price.

But I said that I wouldn't buy it until I had twice the purchase price, and I saw no reason to veer off course. Even though I had absolutely no idea how I was going to make another half million dollars. I mean, it had taken me close to 40 years before I was involved in a deal where I made significant money. But I just knew that the how would somehow be revealed to me.

Several weeks later, my partner in the deal said he found another property that he thought was even better. He suggested that we take everything we had just made and roll it into purchasing the second property. Everything. I can tell you first-hand that when you grow up without money and you make $350,000, it feels like all the money in the world, and you are not in a hurry to risk it. Your natural inclination is to hold onto it with both fists in a monetary death grip. Such a tremendous sum of money represents freedom and safety.

But that, I'm sorry to say, is a poor person's mentality. Rich people think differently. They think that if there is more money to be made, a second investment, albeit a risk, is a smart thing to do provided you've researched it and come to that conclusion. So as hard as it was, I beat back my fear for a second time and reinvested the whole amount.

Six months or so later, we sold the second piece and made even more money. I think my total share was somewhere around $800,000. So I went to check on the price of my house and it had gone down to $425,000.

When selling commercial land, the closing takes a bit of time. So another six months passed before settlement day arrived. I was about to come into a great deal of money, far more than I had ever had in my entire life, and buy my dream vacation home. It had remained for sale the entire time, which was reaching the three-year mark.

Then it disappeared.

I couldn't find the listing anywhere. I called the realtor but all they would tell me was that it was no longer for sale. *How could this happen?* I thought. *Impossible.* That was my house, and there was no way someone was swooping in at the last second to steal it from me.

I identified who the owner was and found out that he owned a restaurant in the same town. I flew to Florida and showed up at his restaurant.

"Is Tony here?" I asked.

The waiter nodded and went to get him. Tony said, "You wanted to see me?"

"I did. I was wondering whatever happened to the house you had for sale a couple of miles from here."

"I couldn't sell it, so I took it off the market."

I pulled out a chair. "Well, why don't you sit down and sell it to me?"

He looked at me like I was crazy, but we did, in fact, sit and discuss the property and the overall real estate market, eventually agreeing on a purchase price of $325,000.

Three years had passed since I first saw a picture of the property on my way to get coffee one morning. It might not be raising $1 million in 24 hours and then meeting Elvis, but it was still a pretty impressive example of how the concept works for anyone who uses it in any circumstance. And I'm begging you not to see this as bragging; I don't tell you to impress you but to impress upon you how this can work for anyone.

Confident clarity and absolute belief mixed with persistence that doesn't recognize failure will yield you all your dreams.

Confident clarity and absolute belief mixed with persistence that doesn't recognize failure will yield you all your dreams.

A word of caution: please don't let the figures throw you. Given that you are just starting out on your journey, it might be hard to relate to stories about land purchases where hundreds of thousands of dollars are at stake. Like my warning to listen to *what* certain success gurus say as opposed to *how* they say it, I don't want you to focus on the figures. I'm telling you that there will be a day in your life when the size of those numbers seem small.

In the movie *Wall Street*, Gordon Gekko talks of making an $800,000 profit on a real estate investment. "At the time I thought it was all the money in the world, and now it's a day's pay."

You will get there too, and when you do you'll be faced with different fears and concerns. You'll go from fears about not having any money to fears about losing what you've accumulated. Please remember what you've read here. Don't give into fear whether your bank account is in the black or the red. Always strive to think like a rich person.

The Takeaway

✔ What you truly believe will happen, will happen.

✔ Persistence and belief have to be inextricably linked.

✔ Don't be overly concerned with the how.

TASK: First of all, reread this chapter. It's that important. Then create an affirmation of something that you want to become a reality within the next six months. Read that affirmation every single morning and believe it will come true.

Small Changes Will Yield Big Results

People often say that motivation doesn't last. Well, neither does bathing—that's why it's necessary daily.

—Zig Ziglar

What you've read so far is the absolute how-to when it comes to attaining money and fulfillment. You could stop reading right now, apply what you've learned, and live a life brimming with success. What follows, though, are 10 tips that will help accelerate the process as you venture forth. Please be mindful that these are things you should do each and every day, not occasionally. Some of these tips are so simple you might be tempted to ignore them. I wouldn't.

1. Gratitude

We all have a tremendous amount to be grateful for. Whether it feels like it or not, you live better than 99 percent of people on earth. Desiring more out of life is great, but it doesn't give any of us the right to ignore what we already have. And this goes hand-in-glove with much of what we've already covered.

When you're grateful, you emit a positive vibe that works to attract even greater happiness. It also helps to always keep you grounded. The whole idea of this book is to search your soul for your life's desire and then scale that mountain with confidence. But it can't just be about reaching the summit.

Gratitude is enjoying the climb, realizing that every step you take brings you closer to your dreams. Said yet another way, wanting what you have is as important as having what you want.

Whenever I write down new goals I always include a sentence that reads something like this: *I am and will remain grateful for everything in my life and will reflect on my good fortune daily.* And I do just that, saying out loud all of the great things I have, from my life to my wife and from my health to my wealth. When you realize how good your life is, you immediately take on a more positive outlook. Being grateful for what you have is in perfect synergy with striving for more; I like to think of gratitude and desire as always being linked together.

The analogy I like best is fly fishing. When you fly fish in a river, you stand on the bow of the boat looking ahead for fish. You have to stay focused ahead of you to see the opportunities when they arrive. But every once in a while, I like to turn around and look out over the rear of the boat, taking in the beauty of where we just came through. The view of the canyons or the mountains or just the bends in the river are really something to behold.

Same is true with life. As you find yourself immersed in your own search for happiness, never forget to take a second to be grateful for where you are, who you are, and for all the terrific things in your life, of which there are many.

2. Try Everything

Remember when I wrote that I have many regrets? This is probably the biggest one of all. I had a narrow mind as a young person and was averse to trying new things. I may have been the greatest sculptor the world has ever known, or the greatest goaltender in hockey history, or an Academy Award-winning actor who only worked three months a year and made $20 million per picture. But I never tried any of those things, and I regret it.

After analyzing my own life, I've come to the conclusion that fear of embarrassment was my personal Achilles' heel. There is absolutely nothing wrong with trying something and determining that it isn't your thing. But avoiding new things simply because of fear is just plain stupid. If ever you find yourself faced with a new endeavor, remember my friend who was afraid to learn how to fly fish and how overcoming that fear changed his life. Try everything; you never know what may light a fire within you.

3. Don't Be Afraid to Be Different

I'm not referring to dyeing your hair purple or wearing flip-flops with a suit. I mean you should think for yourself. Steven Spielberg credits his mother with a great deal of his success because of how she nurtured his talents as a small child. His mother would occasionally allow him to skip school as a child so he could make movies. Of course the movies he made at 10 years old had only one actor in them: his mother.

In essence Mrs. Spielberg said to her son: *It's important that you learn how to do this. In fact, it's so important that I'll let you miss school one day to do it.* She thought differently than most other parents, and it paid off handsomely in the end for Spielberg.

Don't hesitate to think for yourself and follow your passions or help someone else follow theirs. Remember that only your idea of what success is matters. Sometimes looking at things a little differently makes all the difference in the world.

4. Admit Failings

No matter how successful you ultimately wind up being, you will have setbacks and failures along the way. Failing is fine provided that you fail quickly and move on. There is absolutely no shame in failing at anything temporarily. Real failure only occurs when you give up. **You can learn far more from temporary failure than you can from success.** Failures point out the flaws that need to be fixed, changed, tweaked, or figured out.

A good way to think about it is that every finished product is nothing more than the result of overcoming every obstacle you encountered along the way. And the same is true whether we're talking about a product or a person. When you make a mistake, admit it, learn from it, endeavor never to repeat it, and move on.

Sometimes temporary failure is nature's way of saying that you're off course. It's never saying that your destination is wrong, just that you have to find another way to get there. That's how I choose to view what people refer to as failure. It's just pointing out the need for a course correction.

5. Find the Right Friends and Colleagues

Most people are more careful picking out their fruit than their friends. Friends are either helping you get where you want to go, or hindering you from getting there, it's as simple as that. I realize that seems harsh, but I'm dedicated to telling you the truth in this book. I have long believed that if you show me the five people that you spend the most time with, I'll show you your future. If you hang around with positive people, you will become positive; if you hang around with smart people, you'll become smarter; if you hang around with successful people, you can't help but become successful.

But if you choose to spend your time with those who are negative, unintelligent, lazy, unambitious, or lacking character in general, you're doomed. Spending time with wayward people is a lot like smoking cigarettes: it seems cool at first and you don't really notice anything bad happening at the beginning, but it will eventually kill you. This truth carries over into who you choose for your business partners. Choose them carefully and ask yourself: *Will this person help me or hurt me?*

When two or more people are of like mind and share the same desires and drive to attain a goal, they become unstoppable. All of the power that positivity creates is doubled, tripled, and even quadrupled when like-minded people join together in a pursuit.

6. Time Is Generally Not Your Friend

I suggest that you act with urgency when it comes to pursuing your dreams. My father, who I love and admire, told me that his single biggest regret in life was that he always thought he had more time to pursue his passions and his dreams.

Please learn from this mistake.

Today is better than tomorrow in all things.

I always act like I'm running out of time. Today is better than tomorrow in all things. I'm not suggesting that you rush into things without due caution; I'm merely saying that putting off your dreams, hopes, aspirations, or plans is a huge mistake. You don't tend to have more time when you get older, you tend to have less. And Sir Isaac Newton had it right: a body at rest tends to stay at rest. And let's be honest, the number one reason people put off pursuing their passions is—say it with me now—fear.

If we avoid trying, we can never fail. I think from a psychological standpoint, people in general feel that it's better to keep the dream alive than deal with the reality of temporary failure or rejection.

Don't give in to fear.

Fear is nothing more than a bully that will push you around as long as you let it. Don't wind up being one of the people who have a bumper sticker that reads: *I don't regret anything I did, only what I didn't do.* Instead, be the person who went after their dreams, worked hard, persevered, and succeeded. And believe me, nobody puts a bumper sticker on a Bentley.

7. Financial Education

Ever wonder why professional athletes who earned tens of millions of dollars go broke? Because money doesn't make you smarter. You don't necessarily need to understand money in order to attain it, but if you have any hopes of keeping it, you better have a full understanding of it.

The velocity of money, the Principle of 72, 1031

exchanges, qualified investors, real estate investment trusts, short term vs. long term capital gains, cap rate—these are all financial terms that you have to become familiar with if you intend on being in the game. And let me tell you a little secret: they're easy to learn and learning the rules is really the first step toward mastering any game.

There is no shortage of books and videos out there on the subject, but I do think that Robert Kiasaki does a particularly great job with financial education. *Rich Dad, Poor Dad* has sold millions of copies for a reason. It's a great story that explains money in a way that young people in particular can really grasp onto. I highly suggest picking up a copy and delving into the subject.

8. Credit Cards Are Legalized Loan Sharking

Stay away from credit cards when you're young. Revolving debt will keep you enslaved in a way that you can't begin to imagine when you say: *Charge it.* If you have a $5,000 credit card debt and pay the minimum payment every month, it will take you 22 years to pay off the debt. Not to mention that the iPod, new jeans, concert tickets, or whatever comprises your particular debt, will cost you nearly $11,000 over time.

And don't kid yourself; it's easier than you think to rack up debt, and it can be addictive. I've seen people run up $100,000 in credit card debt. Their minimum payments alone are in the thousands, and that's every month. Don't succumb to weakness in this regard. If you can't afford it, don't buy it.

And please just smile and say no, thank you every time a sales clerk says: *You'll get 15 percent off your purchase if you open a charge account with us.* Stop and ask yourself why the company is making you that offer. Because they know that they'll make far more money in interest payments that you'll be forced to make over time. Don't fall for it.

As part of your financial education you'll learn the difference between what's commonly referred to as good debt as opposed to bad debt. This is absolutely essential to creating wealth. In a nutshell, if you create debt in order to make money, it's good debt; if you create debt in order to just buy yourself something, that's bad debt.

Please do yourself a huge favor and stay away from this trap.

9. To-Do Lists Are Awesome

I've stressed the importance of written goals, which you now know are absolutely essential to success. But on a day-in, day-out basis, written to-do lists can play an extremely important role in making you not only successful but really efficient. Take the time every day to list what you want to accomplish. I always do mine in order of importance and for whatever reason I always number them. I try never to go to number two until I accomplish number one.

It's a real feeling of accomplishment when you get to cross off something on your to-do list. It also helps you to effectively move from one task to the next because you've already planned it out in your mind and you can see at a glance what still needs to be done. I have lists all over my desk to this day. I find it to be a terrific tool.

10. Be Generous

I understand that it seems counterintuitive, but the more you give, the more you get. Strive to be generous with people. Most of us, whether we realize it or not, have far more of everything than we actually need. Look for opportunities to be generous to those you meet. I personally think that it's best if done anonymously, but that's totally up to you.

Everything about a truly generous act is uplifting. You feel good, whoever you help feels good—it's the ultimate win-win. If you don't believe me, take some old clothes down to the nearest shelter and see what kind of reception you get. And your generosity need not be limited to just those in need. Do something nice for a family member or neighbor. Every time my wife makes a chicken pot pie at home, she makes one for our elderly neighbor, Mr. Howe. He lives alone, and I've seen his reaction. I think he loves that someone thinks about him enough to make him a meal.

Now here's the key to generosity: never do it to get something back. Just do it to do it. Make someone else happy without expecting anything at all in return. As ludicrous as it may sound, I don't even take a tax deduction for any charitable donation. I just want to do something nice for someone else. Remarkably, though, good things always seem to happen to me whenever I do a charitable act. Again, that is absolutely not the reason I do it, but something great seems to always follow it. I can't explain why, but it always seems to work out that way.

The Takeaway

✔ Make these tools part of your daily life. Each will get you closer to your life's goals. Ideally, you should make every one of these tools part of your daily life without delay. However, if that seems too overwhelming, start with one or two, make them a habit, and then continue adopting the rest one at a time until you have adopted them all.

✔ Simple changes in your daily thinking and the way you approach life can make all the difference in how quickly you attain the future you want.

TASK: We all have a lot to be grateful for. Starting today, make it a habit to say out loud every day how grateful you are for all the things in your life.

Conclusion

So there you have it: a road map to success and happiness. All you have to do is follow it and believe that you'll get there. And please make no mistake about it, belief that you'll attain your dreams is the single greatest asset that you have regardless of what the dream may be. Please let me leave you with one final example of just how powerful this mind-set is.

As I've explained, I make my living as a personal injury attorney. One day I received a call from a former client who told me his 20-year-old son had been involved in a terrible car accident in Florida. I listened as his father explained to me that his son would never walk again because of a spinal cord injury. I went to the airport and flew to see the family.

I've seen a lot in my business, but I have to say walking into that hospital room was one of the hardest things I've ever had to do. Derrik Amaral lay there with a halo collar bolted to his skull and a tube in his mouth that enabled a respirator to breathe for him. CAT scans, MRIs, and X-rays hung on every square inch of wall space. There were doctors and nurses stepping around machinery and around family members who were huddled together talking, praying, or crying.

I was actually standing with Derrik's parents when a

woman in a white lab coat came over and said bluntly that Derrik had a suffered a severe spinal cord injury and he would never walk again. She went on to say that keeping him alive was their short-term goal. She said she was sorry and turned to walk away. There was a feeling of shock in the room, but I couldn't help myself.

"How can you say that?" I asked rather tersely.

The woman turned around. "Well, I can't lie to them. That's the situation, and if he survives, it's something that the whole family will have to learn to live with."

I never raised my voice, but I didn't whisper either. "Well, I believe that he's going to walk again. And I would appreciate it if you didn't say anything to the contrary."

I then turned to Derrik, who couldn't speak at all at this point, and basically repeated myself. "You will walk again. Just repeat it in your mind every day, and then say it out loud every day as you start to get better. And never listen to anyone who says anything else."

Derrik's mother crossed the room to hug me, grateful that someone voiced hope. But when Derrik stared back at me, unable to do anything else, it felt like more than hope. It felt like an understanding. Perhaps an understanding of the very concept I'm hoping to teach you.

Two and a half long years passed. Two and a half years of illnesses, doctor's appointments, therapy, surgeries, and only occasional, minute progress. But Derrik never stopped believing and worked as hard as a person could work toward a goal that seemed all but impossible.

So one day I was scrolling through Facebook, and I saw a video of Derrik and he was standing, unassisted, behind a walker. I clicked on it and watched Derrik Amaral walk for the first time since his accident. He was flanked by his family, nurses, and therapists, all of whom were cheering, clapping, and crying. Only this time they were tears of joy.

I immediately picked up my phone and called his father. "I just saw Derrik walking. Was he really doing that on his own?"

His father, Ernie, could barely get the words out that his son was actually walking on his own. I told him how happy I was for all of them, and that it was nothing short of a miracle.

Ernie then said, "Do you remember what you told the doctor that day in Derrik's hospital room?"

I smiled. "I remember."

"I honestly think that made all the difference. We always appreciated what you said, and Derrik never forgot it. And now, he's walking again."

In all my years as a lawyer, I've never been more proud of anything. And selfishly, it's really what I want most out of this book: I want someone to come up to me or email me someday and say that what they learned in this book made a difference in their life.

I wish you a life filled with passion, happiness, fulfillment, and success.

It dawns on me as I put the finishing touches on this book, that over the last 17 years I've written three books. I rewrote each ten times, had six agents, and have submitted them to dozens and dozens of publishers, yet I haven't sold one. But I will.

Good luck.

About The Author

For the past 23 years Darin Colucci has been a successful trial attorney in Massachusetts, often representing plaintiffs in high profile personal injury cases. In recognition of his work in this field Newsweek.com recently named him one of the ten best personal injury attorneys in America. He is one of the founding partners of Colucci, Colucci, Marcus, & Flavin and makes his home in Duxbury, MA, where he lives with his wife Lorna, and son Jackson. He is a graduate of Bucknell University and Suffolk University Law School where he was a staff member and editor of the law review. He has been a commentator on WBZ radio in Boston and, along with his firm, has been recognized numerous times by the publication *Super Lawyers.*

Darin has also written several works of fiction, been a successful investor, entrepreneur, and inventor who recently designed a safety mechanism to stop wandering in daycare centers and Alzheimer units. In addition, he spent 12 years as a college football coach. During that time, he gave dozens of speeches to young adults on such subjects as success, integrity, mind-set, and the importance of attitude.

Everything I Never Learned in School about How to Be Successful

Darin Colucci

Author website: www.NeverLearnedInSchool.com

Publisher: SDP Publishing

Also available in ebook format

Available at all major bookstores

 **SDP Publishing**

www.SDPPublishing.com

Contact us at: info@SDPPublishing.com

CPSIA information can be obtained
at www.ICGtesting.com
Printed in the USA
LVOW04s2322201116
513849LV00006B/34/P

9 780997 722475